FANNY
AND
ALEXANDER

FANNY AND ALEXANDER

Ingmar Bergman

Translated from the Swedish by Alan Blair

PANTHEON BOOKS
New York

All rights reserved under International and Pan-American Copyright Conventions. Published in the United States by Pantheon Books, a division of Random House, Inc., New York, and simultaneously in Canada by Random House of Canada Limited, Toronto. Originally published in Sweden as *Fanny och Alexander* by Norstedt & Soner Forlag. Copyright © 1979 by Ingmar Bergman.

Library of Congress Cataloging in Publication Data

Bergman, Ingmar, 1918–
Fanny and Alexander.

Screenplay for the motion picture of the same name.
Translation of: Fanny och Alexander.
I. Fanny och Alexander (Motion picture) II. Title.
PN1997.F32713 1983   791.43'72   81–47188
ISBN 0–394–52070–X
ISBN 0–394–74945–6 (pbk.)

The photographs throughout this book
were taken by Arne Carlsson.

Manufactured in the United States of America

FIRST AMERICAN EDITION

FANNY
AND
ALEXANDER

Characters

MRS. HELENA EKDAHL, née Mandelbaum, widow, former
   actress

  OSCAR EKDAHL, her eldest son, theatrical manager

  EMILIE EKDAHL, his wife, actress

  AMANDA   aged 12 ⎞

  ALEXANDER aged 10 ⎬   their children

  FANNY   aged 8 ⎠

  CARL EKDAHL, professor, her second son

  LYDIA EKDAHL, his wife, German-born

  GUSTAV ADOLF EKDAHL, restaurant-keeper, businessman,
    her third son

  ALMA EKDAHL, his wife

  PETRA aged 18 ⎫

  JENNY aged 8 ⎬ their children

EVA, aged 7, a girl living next door

VEGA, Helena's cook

ESTER, Helena's parlor maid

ALIDA and LISEN, cooks

SIRI and BERTA, housemaids

MAJ, Emilie and Oscar's lame nursemaid

ISAK JACOBI, Jew, businessman

ARON   aged about 20 ⎫

ISMAEL aged about 16 ⎬ the Jew's nephews

AT THE THEATER

FILIP LANDAHL, aged 73, producer and actor *(père noble)*
HANNA SCHWARTZ, ingenue
MIKAEL BERGMAN, young, promising, plays Hamlet
HARALD MORSING, Claudius in *Hamlet*
TOMAS GRAAL, plays Orsino in *Twelfth Night*
JOHAN ARMFELDT, plays Malvolio
GRETE HOLM, plays Maria
MR. SALENIUS, plays Sir Toby Belch
MRS. SINCLAIR, asthmatic, in the box office
THE PROMPTER
THE BUSINESS MANAGER
MRS. PALMGREN, office worker
THE PROPERTY MANAGER
DR. FÜRSTENBERG, family doctor
THE COLONEL
THE CHANCELLOR OF THE UNIVERSITY
BISHOP EDVARD VERGÉRUS
   HENRIETTA VERGÉRUS, the bishop's sister
   BLENDA VERGÉRUS, the bishop's mother
   ELSA BERGIUS, the bishop's aunt
   MALLA TANDER, cook, ratlike
   KARNA ⎫
   SELMA ⎬ housemaids
   JUSTINE ⎭
   THE CARETAKER
   THE COACHMAN, addicted to drink
   PAULINE   aged 12 ⎫
   ESMERALDA aged 10 ⎭ ghosts
AN OLD CLERGYMAN
A POLICE SUPERINTENDENT
A BRIBED CLERGYMAN
ROSA, a nursemaid

I—Prologue

A river with a fairly swift current and several small cataracts and waterfalls flows through the town. On a steep eminence lies the castle, a large medieval pile, the residence of the governor. In the midst of a meekly monotonous cluster of houses stands the cathedral, a monument to the piety of a bygone age—there the bishop fulminates. The town also boasts a university heavy with tradition and a theater, where plays are performed every day of the week. Other amenities include a newly erected hotel, showy rather than handsome, two small, industrious horse-drawn trams that crisscross the town, an unpretentious railway station, a district with stone houses for the well-to-do and the professors, and one with ramshackle dwellings for artisans, students, and day laborers. Shipping on a modest scale plies the river, while industry comprises a couple of good-sized mills that grind the corn from the fertile plain. There is also a smelly tannery with a shoe factory attached to it. A shady park and a famous botanical garden complete the picture of unassuming prosperity, solid self-esteem, and rather sleepy cultural and scientific activity. It is a world unto itself, worrying very little about the storms and portents of the times. The new dogmas and the revolutionary ideas are heatedly discussed in drafty student lodgings reeking of paraffin. Otherwise the town lives untroubled by the world. The local newspaper keeps an eye on law and order, considering it an obvious duty not to alarm the six thousand loyal subscribers.

Life follows a definite rhythm. In winter the town lives normally, in spring it is seized by a strange excitement, in summer it sleeps peacefully, to be awakened in September by the autumn rains sweeping over the plain and by the students' noisy entry into lecture rooms, lodgings, and eating places. The theater opens its season and the academic orchestra tunes its instruments, the students in the choir clear their throats with pea soup and hot punch, the schoolchildren make their way in misty morning hours through the wet streets strewn with leaves, the professors mount their desks, and the town's own extremely respectable brothel is once again visited by the officers of the nearby garrison. Then comes the winter. In November the first snow falls, a bitter wind blows from the north, the town's aging widows catch cold and die of pneumonia. On Sundays the funeral bells toll under the iron gray sky. Like beetles sluggish with the cold, crapulous students crawl through the snowdrifts to the eating place to get a hair of the dog, and to warm themselves by the stove. Now and then a sleigh jingles with false gaiety through the streets. There is a dull roar from the cataracts, and the black water swirls along between the edges of the ice; it is the hour for life-weary suicides. At the theater the great tragedies are performed and smoke from the wooden stoves hangs like a mist above the roofs weighted with snow. Suddenly one day it is spring; there it is, swathed in its chill white light, invincible. The town lives in a fever of activity. The students go up for their exams and defend their doctor's theses, one ball succeeds the other in a whirl of festivity. The pawnbrokers are kept busy: The winter coats are put away and the tailcoats are taken out. The little old ladies who have survived the winter adorn the cemetery or the park; it is time for weddings and boundless expectations. The gardens are a froth of fruit blossom and lilac, the girl students wear light dresses, the brass band from the garrison gives a concert nearly every evening, and the inevitable English drawing room comedy is given at the theater.

Then one day the town falls asleep. All is quiet; even the roar of the cataracts sinks to a murmur. The days are long, the evenings still. The students are on summer vacation; the well-to-do hang sheets at the windows and spread dustcovers over the furniture, wrap the chandeliers in tulle, and roll up the carpets. They go to their summer cottages by the sea. The less well-to-do move out to their small gardens on the plain or to rich relations on the big estates. The great bell of the cathedral measures the quarters and the hours; the sunlight blazes down on empty streets. On the white benches in the esplanade sit those who are left behind, the lonely ones. The town sleeps without stirring in the white heat over the plain.

This is the town's rhythm and breathing; most of those who live in it think it is a good town, the best imaginable. They are not worried about the future and have no reason to be ashamed of the past. The general opinion is that the authorities rule with wisdom. The king protects the authorities' decisions and watches over the citizens' safety. God, finally, holds his hand over the king, and the waltz from *The Merry Widow* is played as a duet in almost every family that owns a piano.

II

The theater was built at the beginning of the nineteenth century and will soon be a hundred years old. Several wealthy townsmen who had a passion for forest walks, cold baths, and culture clubbed together and defrayed the cost of the temple. Splendor and dilapidation succeeded each other. Early in the 1860s the place was bought by a prosperous businessman, Oscar Ekdahl, who had just married a prominent young actress from the capital. He was a wise and broad-minded man and let his wife take over the running of the theater, on condition that she herself did not perform. A son was born who was also given the name of Oscar. Unlike his mother he became a rather mediocre actor. When he married a drama student in 1889, his mother retired and handed over the management to the young couple. She was left a widow a year later and divided the large handsome apartment in the square by putting up a wall in the middle of the dining room. The young couple moved into the sunnier part of the house. The wife made rapid progress in her profession, in a few years becoming a famous actress. Her husband managed the theater with competence and care. A small but good company was engaged. Their activities flourished and were even spoken of in the capital. Oscar and Emilie enjoyed a modest happiness, their only sorrow being that the marriage was childless for more than ten years. Then three children were born in quick succession: Amanda, Alexander, and Fanny. Of this and much else I shall speak later.

At the time of our film the theater is well run but rather old-fashioned. True, electric lighting has been installed on the stage and in the auditorium, but that is all. Newfangled things like spotlights and rheostats are unknown aids. The old stage lighting is quite sufficient: floats and battens with small sleepy bulbs in different colors. The stage still consists of broad knotty planks with a steep rake from the back wall to the prompter's box. Up in the dark flies hang aged forests, stormy seas, low farmhouses, stately banqueting halls, and one or two terrifying dragons that no one has the heart to get rid of. The actors' dressing rooms are on two levels next to the stage, the women's to the right and the men's to the left. The managerial offices are squashed into three small rooms just inside the stage door. Oscar Ekdahl prefers to receive his guests in his private dressing room, the only one with running water and tolerably comfortable furniture. Under the sloping stage are two cellars, one on top of the other. They contain antiquated and now discarded wooden machinery for scene changes, trapdoors, and other mysterious things. In the upper cellar, on endless shelves, the properties are kept. The furniture is stored in the lower cellar and is shifted by means of a quaint old lift that is worked by hand. In one corner of the bottom cellar is a heavy iron grating, under which is a stream of swirling black water, apparently bottomless. A horrible crime is connected with this water and this grating, possibly also a ghost. In the back wall are two high, narrow windows; sometimes in the afternoons, when rehearsals are over, the caretaker opens the shutters. The sunlight strikes in with long, slender, sharply defined rays and the fine stage dust spins in the draft. All is quiet, as the back of the theater opens onto a yard with a few shady trees. Now and then a bird flies in by mistake. Flapping in fright and cheeping incessantly it rises into the dark toward the catwalk and the blackened rafters. When the bird is silent the stillness becomes magic: Voices then silenced can now be heard; beingless shadows and the imprints of fierce passions can be glimpsed. The dusty air, cut through by the sword blades of sunlight, grows thick with voices long since mute and movements that have ceased.

The curtain is of canvas and made to look like material draped in huge folds and adorned with braids and gold tassels. The back of it is gray and patched, crossed with narrow wooden slats. At eye level is a peephole so that the actors, themselves unseen, can watch and count their audience. To the left the stage manager has his little cubbyhole with bells and speaking tubes as well as two ropes, one for the howling of the wind, the other for the rumbling of the thunder. Wafting above the stage is an ineradicable smell of dust, smoking stoves, and dead mice.

The auditorium is intimate and shaped like a horseshoe; it contains stalls with sixteen rows of seats upholstered in shabby red plush, a dress circle, an upper circle, and a gallery. The dress circle is divided into boxes, each having six chairs and its own entrance. The upper circle has narrow wooden benches covered with red cloth. The gallery has standing room only, but it costs a mere trifle and you can bring your own chair if you like. To right and left of the proscenium are two elegant and spacious boxes. One is reserved for the theater's board of directors and the other for the governor and the mayor—or the king, if he should take it into his head to visit the town's playhouse, something that has never yet occurred.

On the ceiling of the auditorium are paintings by a famous son of the town. They show the Greek gods tumbling among the clouds, paying homage to a young Thalia, who bears the soft regular features of Helena Mandelbaum. This is the elder Oscar Ekdahl's tribute to his wife and it cost him several thousand riksdaler, a fact that he often pointed out with pride. Round the divine scene hang six chandeliers, which give the theater a mild and beautifying glow. The difference between the front of the house and backstage is marked. Out here everything is spic and span and well cared for. Behind the scenes it is dirty, dusty, and dilapidated.

Provision has also been made for bodily well-being. On a level with the dress circle and with a view over the square is the restaurant, which is run by Oscar's younger brother, Gustav Adolf Ekdahl. Here the dishes are so appetizing, the drinks so exactly the right temperature, and the waiters so obliging that some theatergoers prefer Gustav Adolf's material edification to his brother's more intellectual one. At times the hilarity is so great that a drama student is sent as express messenger to request moderation of the mirth, which is seriously disturbing a famous soliloquy or a very moving scene. Otherwise the brothers are on most affectionate terms.

Finally a word about the audience. There is a performance every evening for eight months (the theater is closed on Christmas Day, Good Friday, and Easter Sunday). The program is changed every four weeks, and on the whole the same people come to see all nine plays. It is a faithful if conservative audience. Oscar Ekdahl is chary of making experiments. Strindberg and Ibsen are regarded with the utmost suspicion and are therefore seldom performed.

III

When the elder Oscar Ekdahl married Helena Mandelbaum, he bought not only the theater but also a handsome brick house on the other side of the square. The family moved into the top floor, which was furnished with every conceivable convenience. They kept open house, and Helena was always surrounded by a swarm of admirers. When Oscar died, his widow suggested that the apartment should be divided into two halves. This was done by putting up a wall in the middle of the spacious dining room. In the wall was an almost invisible jib-door, shaded by a tall tiled stove on one side and a massive sideboard on the other. The door was never used by the grown-up members of the family.

So the younger Oscar Ekdahl and his pretty wife Emilie moved into the sunnier side of the apartment that looked out on the town park with its shady elms, lush lawns, flower beds, fountains, and statues.

Relations between the young family on one side of the door and the mother-in-law on the other side were at first polite but hardly cordial.

One of the reasons for the coolness was the big refurnishing. The newlyweds had spent their lengthy honeymoon traveling on the Continent, eagerly interested in all they saw. In this way they had discovered a new style of furniture, which they liked and wanted to bring home. Oscar, though an unassuming man and a poor actor, knew his own mind and had the faculty of realizing his ideas. To his mother's dismay the old furniture was relegated to the storeroom of the theater. Painters, upholsterers, plumbers, and electricians got busy. Bright-colored walls, light curtains in clear prints with floral patterns and simple drapings, a spacious bathroom with water heater and water closet were the result of their efforts. Linoleum in cheerful colors was tacked over the old scrubbed boards, and rugs in gay patterns were unrolled over dark and creaking parquet floors. To crown it all there was new furniture in pure art nouveau, designed by a specially engaged interior decorator. The light was given free play; there was space and air in the old apartment, which was changed beyond recognition.

Helena Ekdahl noted these alterations in polite silence, suspecting a belated rebellion against parental authority, which indeed it was. She blamed her daughter-

in-law for this, but never brought the matter up. Oscar
also tried to persuade his mother to install central heating and dismantle the old-fashioned tiled stoves. Here,
however, he failed. To his astonishment she burst into
tears and said that he obviously no longer loved her.
Oscar could see no connection between central heating
and his love for his mother but let the matter drop. In
due course a telephone was put in and the two families
could, without meeting, inquire about each other's
health and other topics. There was never any hostility
except between the two cooks, who were outstanding
artists and personalities to reckon with. Helena's cook
was old. No one knew her exact age; she had been
handed down in the Ekdahl family, burdened with
knowledge and traditions. The other cook was a robust
middle-aged woman with modern ideas about upbringing and food. So long as the young Ekdahls had no children, the two rivals maintained a dour, charitable neu-
trality. When the children began running to and fro
between the kitchens, a bitter and long-suppressed enmity flared up, lasting until Alexander's twelfth birthday, when old Vega died all of a sudden, bent over the
half-finished cake.

In the autumn of 1895, Emilie Ekdahl went to Helsinki
to fulfill an engagement as guest artist. A year later, after
ten years of childlessness, she was delivered of a daughter, who was christened Amanda.

A young and very talented actor with a romantic ap-
pearance joined the company. *The Lady of the Camellias*
was to be given with Emilie as the unfortunate courtesan
and Mr. Palmlund as the fiery Armand. It was one of the
theater's biggest successes and ran for forty-six perfor-
mances, which was unusual. The new actor received an
engagement in the capital and word went round that
Emilie had been seen with disheveled hair and eyes red
with weeping. She gave birth to a son, who was called

Alexander. He was small and weakly and was hastily baptized at the hospital, but he gradually recovered under his mother's tender care.

A year later Fanny was born, healthy and plump and very like the archbishop, who had paid a visit to the diocese.

The rapid increase in the Ekdahl family gave rise to gossip in the town, while those immediately concerned appeared very happy. As both Oscar and Emilie were generally liked, tongues soon stopped wagging and the sight of the flourishing mother with her well-kept and merry children gave pleasure to all.

The grandmother had noted Amanda's birth without any emotion to speak of. She took all the greater interest, however, in Alexander's critical beginnings. It was also Alexander who in a reckless moment ventured to open the door between the two apartments. An enticing and rather frightening world extended in front of him. True, he had often been to see his grandmother, but these visits had always been regulated by definite ritual behavior. Now, on this bright, quiet Sunday morning, he could explore. Grandmamma was at church with Vega and Ester. The apartment was empty. The parquet floor creaked under his cautious footsteps. The massive dining table towered over his head. He sat down, leaning against one of its bulbous legs. His brown pinafore with the red borders had a pocket, on which a cat was embroidered. He put both hands in the pocket. He felt safer like that. It was cold too.

The winter's day was sunny and frosty outside the double windows with their patterned screens and heavy draperies. The chairs round the table and walls were upholstered in dark gilt leather, which had a pungent smell. Behind him the sideboard rose up like a castle; glass carafes and crystal bowls gleamed in the space between the two towers. On the wall to the left hung a picture showing white, red, and yellow houses above blue water; on the water strange boats were sailing. The grandfather clock, which reached almost to the ornamented ceiling, muttered crossly to itself.

From where he sat he could see into the gleaming green drawing room—green walls, carpets, furniture, curtains. There were also several palms growing in green urns. He glimpsed the naked white lady with the chopped-off arms. She stood leaning forward a little and regarding Alexander thoughtfully. He had seen her many times before but could never make up his mind if he was to think of her as a little bit alive and therefore frightening but at the same time attractive in some way. Now that he was alone here with her, the naked lady was very much alive—he could feel it in his tummy. On the curved bureau with the brass fittings and feet stood a heavy ormolu clock under its glass dome. A man playing the flute leaned against the dial and on a stone sat a lady in a low-cut bodice, large hat, and short, wide skirt; they too were of gilt. When the clock struck twelve, the man played his flute and the little lady danced. Grandmamma had often shown Alexander the mechanism, but alone here now it was all different. He felt sorry for the man and woman shut up under a glass dome.

Grandmamma has gotten up late this Sunday morning. The big bed with its tall ornamented ends is still unmade, and the pillows smell of Grandmamma's nice rose scent (it is called "glycerine and rose water" and can be bought quite simply at the pharmacy, but Alexander did not know that). The room is not particularly big. The furnishings have not been changed for over forty years; everything is much the same as it was on the wedding day in 1862, when Helena and Oscar Ekdahl climbed into the marital bed for the first time. In it they took their pleasure for more than twenty years; in it they wept, bickered, and held each other's hands, or perhaps talked sensibly of the theater's repertoire, the children's future, the mother-in-law's temper, and their friends' misfortunes. The elder Oscar Ekdahl and his wife Helena, née Mandelbaum, lived in what they themselves considered a happy marriage, and their mutual loyalty was never shaken.

On the wall facing the bed, illumined by the winter light, hangs a painting of Helena as Iphigenia. A strange radiance emanates from it. Alexander imagines that his grandmother moves inside the picture; he can almost hear her speaking. His mother has played the part, and he knows the words by heart. He delights in her well-shaped hands; the soft lips; the heavy, firm breasts under the transparent dress; the grave, irregularly formed eyes; the broad, clear brow; and the curly black hair. Little else can be said of this room other than that it is cluttered with pictures, photographs, and treasured odds and ends. Grandmamma's bedroom is never really light and it is almost impossible to clean. Twice a year the furniture is taken out, carpets and draperies are beaten, the floor is scrubbed, and the bric-a-brac is polished, but after a few days everything is as dusty as before. The scent of rose water mixed with the smell of aging wood and decomposing velvet hangs heavily in the long dusky room. By the far wall stands a rounded sofa covered with dark red rather threadbare brocade. On it are a lot of variously shaped cushions, all soft and yielding. Helena Ekdahl likes to sit on this sofa with her grandson. There they sit, each clasping a cushion, talking of life and art but also of death and life after this.

A long dark passage with a lofty ceiling goes through the apartment. The insufficient light it gets comes from the rooms on either side and from fanlights above the doors to the kitchen and the servants' room. At the angle of the passage is a secret room. The door has five holes bored in it just above the floor and the walls are covered with red material. On them hang some framed colored pictures representing knights' castles and beautiful damsels in billowing wimples. In the middle of the cramped square room stands a throne with arms and back; it too is covered with red material and has brass fittings on the corners and sides. The seat can be lifted, and under it is a black hole, a bottomless pit, Alexander thinks. Here Grandmamma sits for a long time, groaning and sighing. Alexander has once or twice offered to keep her company in order to divert her, but she has always declined. Alexander's father says Grandmamma suffers from constipation because she is stingy. Vega or Ester never sit for long on the throne. They scurry in, rustle their skirts, and are out again before you can count up to ten.

In the passage stands a large iron stove that gives out its special rather acrid smell of burning coal; the hot iron smells too. In the kitchen Vega is preparing dinner— good nourishing cabbage soup. Warm and unmistakable, the smell spreads through the whole apartment, mingling with the extremely physical odors from the secret room in the angle of the passage. For a small person like Alexander, whose nose is so near the floor, the carpets smell strongly of naphthalene, which soaks into them as they lie rolled up during the summer months. Every Friday, Ester and Vega clean the old parquet with floor polish and turpentine; the reek is overpowering. The knotty floorboards smell of soft soap. The linoleum is cleaned with an ill-smelling mixture of sour skimmed milk and water.

People smell in different ways. Their clothes smell not only of material but of cooking, sweat, tobacco, and perfume. Their shoes smell of leather, boot polish, and foot sweat. People go around as a whole symphony of odors: powder, tar soap, urine, sex, dirt, pomade. Some smell of human being in general, some smell safe, and others smell menacing. Ester, the housemaid, wears a wig, which she sticks on to her bare scalp with a special kind of glue. Ester smells of glue all over. Grandmamma smells of withering roses. Alexander's mother smells as sweet as vanilla; but when she is angry, the down on her upper lip grows moist and she exudes a barely perceptible but pungent odor that tells of danger. A young, plump, red-haired servant girl called Maj, one of whose legs is shorter than the other, is Alexander's favorite smell. He likes nothing so much as to lie in her bed on her arm, his nose pressed to her coarse linen. She smells of sweat and other nice things. Both are aware that such a thing is probably forbidden, but no one has discovered them and they can go on being together like two small, friendly animals. Alexander's elder sister smells of metal; it is odd, but she smells exactly like the pewter bowl on the smoking table in the library. Fanny smells of fresh cream and babies, although she has turned eight.

If you stand under the chandelier in the drawing room with your feet sunk in the endless leaf pattern of the carpet, if you stand quite still and hold your breath, you can hear the silence, which consists of many components: above all the singing of the blood in your eardrums, but also the clocks ticking everywhere, ticking and striking, all at once. Then the roar of the fire in the tiled stove and the faint rattle of the iron doors. Far away a piano can be heard—the girl next door is practicing scales. The sound is barely audible, yet it gives you a twinge of sadness; there is no telling *why*. At the writing table in the library Grandmamma sits bent over her accounts; the steel nib scratches against the paper. From the kitchen you can hear the clatter of dishes and Vega's voice. Then all is silent, except for the swash of the china and silver in the sink.

The winter's day is closing in. A sleigh drives past, bells jingling, horses' hooves clopping against the frozen snow, runners hissing. The clock in the cathedral tower strikes four quarters and the hour of three. *Why am I so sad?* Alexander thinks, standing there on the drawing room carpet. *Why am I so sad? Is it Death, keeping so still out in the semidarkness of the hall? Can I hear his quick, hoarse breathing? Has he come to get Grandmamma as she sits in the library writing in her blue account book?* Alexander wants to run to her and cry in her lap, but he mustn't. If he moves, if he so much as lifts a finger, Death will streak in and get there ahead of him. It turns into a wearisome fight between Alexander and Death. Suddenly Ester starts tipping lumps of coal into the iron stove with a black shovel. The noise breaks the spell, and the grisly guest vanishes.

The dusk deepens and turns blue, filtered through the heavy folds of the curtains. Grandmamma gets up from the writing table and fetches the paraffin lamp. Her son has given her an electric table lamp of iron with a green china shade, but Grandmamma has put it away in the big cupboard and still uses the same paraffin lamp that shone over Oscar's desk at the theater. She lights the yellow flame, turns up the wick, and replaces the chimney and shade. There is a smell of paraffin. Grandmamma's shadow is outlined on the backs of the books. The carbon-filament lamps glow in the hall and the drawing room, leaving a lot of darkness for shadows. The twilight deepens still more. The lamplighter with his pole tramps cautiously along the icy pavement. Now he is lighting the gas lamps in the street. They cast shadows on the ceiling of the drawing room. Alexander can make out seas and mountains, heathens and monsters. Grandmamma turns her face toward him; he cannot see her eyes. She stretches out her hand and asks in a gentle voice if he would like to play cards for a while before dinner.

I must also say a few words about the yard behind

the Ekdahls' house. Opening onto the street at the front is an arched gateway, which at night is closed by heavy oak doors. The ground is paved with cobblestones, and the clatter of horses' hooves and carriages driving into the yard through the archway echoes through the house. There has long been talk of asphalting the entrance, but nothing is ever done. The yard is irregular and extensive, enclosed by a simple three-storied dwelling-house at right angles to the front building, a row of coach houses, stables, and washhouses, as well as a fireproof wall. The town park can be glimpsed through an opening. The ground is only partly paved. In the middle of the yard grows a tall chestnut tree. Two carpet-beating racks stick up like medieval instruments of torture. A covered-over well with a hand pump stands guard by the stables.

Helena Ekdahl keeps a saddle horse, a carriage horse, two gleaming black coupés, and a sleigh, together with a coachman in livery and a groom, who is the coachman's son. They live in two small rooms above the stables. In one of the coach houses stands Oscar's Daimler. It is used only in the summer; Oscar is an enthusiastic but uncertain automobile driver. In the two washhouses there is a constant to-ing and fro-ing of cross mothers and pale children. Steam comes out of the open doors and windows, and the loud voices never stop. A small firm of carriers has rented the rest of the yellow ramshackle row. Business is conducted by three middle-aged brothers and four lean mares. The brothers live with a swarthy housekeeper in the attic of the dwelling-house. The housekeeper has an interesting reputation and six children, all equally thin, pastyfaced, and sniffly with chronic colds.

On the ground floor, to the right of the entrance staircase, is a remarkable shop and a remarkable shopkeeper. He is a lanky man with a stooping gait and large pale hands. He has a long beard, curls at his ears, black eyes, and a narrow white forehead. He wears a greasy hat with a curved brim. His name is Isak Jacobi, and he dines with Helena Ekdahl every Thursday. Ester says he is a dirty disgusting Jew, and she tells Alexander with relish that Isak Jacobi slaughters little children and drinks their blood. Alexander does not believe a word of it, but Ester's tales certainly add to the attraction of Isak's already mysterious person. The shop has a magic of its own. You enter through a door with glass panes and a little bell rings. Isak Jacobi sits by the counter in a black rocking chair, usually reading a book with unfamiliar letters. Fanny and Alexander like going to the Jew's shop. Amanda never goes; she says it smells nasty and that there is a rotting corpse in a back room. This is partly true. Isak Jacobi is the owner of a mummy, which rests in a glass case in the little inner room where he has collected his most precious possessions. Fanny and Alexander always want to see the mummy. It is horrible; the face has been freed from the gold mask and the bandages, and you can see the hair, the ears, the almost corroded lips, the smiling mouth, and the long, crumbling nose. The shop premises extend into the building; there are several rooms with dirty, partly boarded-up windows covered with dusty hangings. On long shelves, on big tables, on the floor, and dangling from the ceiling are thousands of objects of the most varied kinds. No one has ever heard of the Jew selling anything in his shop. Nor has anyone seen him buying anything. It is all a mystery.

The pattern in the yard is constantly changing as humans and animals come and go. The sparrows squabble in the chestnut tree or feast on the horse-droppings, innumerable fat cats live a comfortable vagabond life among rats and mice, children and dogs tumble on the gravel and the withered, ill-kept grass. The caretaker and the odd-job man booze behind the outside privy to the accompaniment of sharp-tongued comments from the women in the brewhouse.

The Ekdahl children are forbidden to play in the yard. In the charge of the lame but cheerful Maj they must march off to the town park, where playmates and sand-pits befitting their station are to be found.

I—Christmas

Ever since the days of the elder Oscar Ekdahl it has been the tradition on Christmas Eve, at one o'clock in the afternoon, to perform *The Play about the Joyful Birth of Christ.* By the same tradition, this performance is just as well attended as the early service in the cathedral on Christmas Day. Even Bishop Edvard Vergérus is present, together with Mayor Falström, Governor Pansarstierna, Rector Magnificus Adam Boetius, and many other prominent citizens with all their households.

(The actors have come to the end, with MARY *and* JOSEPH *in the stall and the* CHILD *asleep in the manger. Celestial music is heard, the stage is flooded with light, and a whiterobed angel, surrounded by cherubs, is lowered from the flies. For a good many years past, the First Lady of the theater,* EMILIE EKDAHL, *has appeared in this important part. The cherubs are played by her children* AMANDA, ALEXANDER, *and* FANNY *with their cousin* JENNY. *When the angels have come to rest on a little bridge near the roof of the stall,* JOSEPH *awakens. He is portrayed modestly but with dignity by the manager of the theater,* OSCAR EKDAHL. *This too is a tradition and* OSCAR *submits to it)*

ANGEL   Worthy Joseph, do not fear,
Thy angel is thee ever near.

This I would that thou shouldst know,
She watches over weal and woe.
I come in haste to bring thee word
From thy creator and thy God.
Mary and the child now wake
And quickly into safety take.
Herod with his murdering hand
Threatens every man-child in this land.

JOSEPH   All this I have noted well
And shall do as you foretell.
Praised be God upon his throne
Who thus protects my only son.

(All the performers come on stage. The orchestra plays a few bars of a Christmas carol. EMILIE *has gathered the four children round her and turns to the audience with a smile)*

EMILIE   Thus, good people, ends our play,
It all ends well this holy day.
The son of God, saved from the sword,
Is our Saviour, Christ the Lord.
We know that in his mercy mild
He guards every woman, man, and child.

(The VIRGIN MARY, *played by* HANNA SCHWARTZ, *holds out her arms in an all-embracing gesture. She has been the theater's ingenue for the last three years and is very popular, especially among elderly men)*

HANNA   A time of joyous Christmas cheer
We wish to all, both far and near.

(It is now the turn of the theater's oldest and foremost actor, FILIP LANDAHL, *who is seventy-three. He fiddles with a scrap*

of paper with his lines on it [short speeches in verse are the very devil])

    FILIP   Merrily may every light
Shed its radiance clear and bright.

*(*ALEXANDER EKDAHL *steps forward. He is ten years old, pale, thin, and nearsighted. His hair is rather sparse. He has a large nose, dark blue eyes, and a wide mouth, which is apt to twist into an embarrassed smile)*

    ALEXANDER *(Clearing his throat)*   Let no one into
    darkness fall,
A Happy Christmas one and all.

(The curtain falls to loud applause, which ends abruptly however, since everyone is in a hurry to get home to their own Christmas celebrations. When the curtain has been lowered for the last time, the actors turn their faces to the wings on the right. GUSTAV ADOLF EKDAHL, *beaming with goodwill and high blood pressure, marches in closely followed by four well-starched waitresses with trays of sweets and four waiters carrying bowls of hot punch and mulled wine. Last comes* ALMA EKDAHL (GUSTAV ADOLF's *stately wife) together with their nineteen-year-old daughter* PETRA, *a copy of her good-humored mother. Between them they are lugging an open leather trunk full of Christmas presents for the theater staff and their families.*

All are now assembled—the actors in their costumes, the stagehands in their Sunday best, the wardrobe mistress with the seamstresses and wigmakers, the women from the box office, and the grave men from the office. It is quite a big company—thirty-four adults and thirteen children. OSCAR EKDAHL *mounts the steps to* JOSEPH *and* MARY's *crib. They all gather round him, clutching their glasses. The manager of the theater is going to make his Christmas speech. His father was a witty, outstanding after-dinner speaker and his Christmas address was one of the highlights of the season. The son is no orator, but he is generally esteemed, and the Christmas speech must be delivered)*

OSCAR   Dear friends, dear fellow workers, dear family! For twenty-two years I have stood here and made a speech. I'm not really any good at this sort of thing. . . .

(OSCAR *looks about him, smiling shrewdly, and they all smile back at him effortlessly, as they think he is a jolly good sort)*

OSCAR *(Thoughtfully)*   . . . at this sort of thing. My only talent, if you can call it talent in my case, is that I love this little world inside the thick walls of this playhouse. And I'm fond of the people who work in this little world. Outside is the big world, and sometimes the little world succeeds for a moment in reflecting the big world, so that we understand it better. Or is it perhaps that we give the people who come here the chance of forgetting for a while. . . .

(He gazes at his glass, which he is holding between both hands. The only sound is the faint howl of the snowstorm up in the darkness of the flies. When he looks up again they can all see that he is unusually pale and has tears in his eyes)

OSCAR   . . . forgetting for a while the harsh world outside. Our theater is a small room of orderliness, routine, conscientiousness, and love. I don't know why I'm so awfully moved today of all days. I feel so comically solemn. I can't explain *how* I feel. I had better be brief.

(He shakes his head, raises his glass, and looks at the people gathered around him)

OSCAR   My mother and I, my wife and my children, wish you all a happy and joyous Christmas. I hope we meet again on Boxing Day, strengthened in body and soul. Merry Christmas!

GUSTAV ADOLF   Merry Christmas, Oscar! Merry Christmas, Emilie!

(Everyone toasts the EKDAHL *family and each other)*

II

(The EKDAHLS *now struggle across the square in a blinding snowstorm, which seems to come from all points of the compass. Drifts have piled up. Three sleighs glide past with hilarious merrymakers on their way to a Christmas party. They are holding torches, the bells jingle, the horses' nostrils are steaming. Opposite the theater the* EKDAHLS' *house is aglow. Arches of lighted candles are in every window.*

In HELENA EKDAHL'*s apartment the preparations for the Christmas dinner are complete. The tree has been lighted, the candelabra, chandeliers, and bracket lamps are glittering, the wood is blazing in the tiled stoves.*

VEGA *and* ESTER *have attired themselves in black silk, starched white aprons, and tall lace caps on top of elaborately dressed hair.*

HELENA *has arrayed herself in a dark red brocade dress, heavy jewelry, and her royal orders. Her hair, though streaked with gray, is still dark and glossy. Her skin is white and gleaming, the dark blue eyes are sharp and clear, the hands soft with no wrinkles or spots.*

She is now standing by the balcony window, watching her large family—her sons, daughters-in-law, and grandchildren —battle through the blizzard down in the square, laughing and shouting. The lights in the theater go out one by one, and soon it is in darkness. The heavy gaslamps outside the main entrance move in the wind and the flames flicker.

Loud voices announce the arrival of HELENA's *eldest son,* PROFESSOR CARL EKDAHL, and his wife, LYDIA. *They wrangle out in the hall, but* CARL's *face lights up as he enters the room and sees his mother. He greets her boisterously. He is a tall, corpulent man, almost bald but with a large beard and side-whiskers. His wife is a fat, meddlesome German woman, who despite her twenty years in the country has not learned the language. She has a fresh complexion, ample bust, and big teeth and is always in a good mood, even when she quarrels.* CARL *and* LYDIA *are childless but lavish their affection on eight allegedly pedigreed cats. Their arms are full of Christmas presents, which are handed over to* ESTER *and put in a large clothes basket, which is already filled to the brim with brightly colored packages.*

*   LYDIA *greets her mother-in-law effusively;* HELENA's *response is friendly but restrained.* CARL *has lighted a cigar and poured himself a brandy. The professor is a heavy drinker but fairly popular with his students.*

*   ISAK JACOBI *now makes his entrance, beaming with delight. His tailcoat is immaculate, his hair and beard are freshly trimmed, and his black eyebrows have been given a neat upward twist. With his nasal bass voice he compliments* HELENA *on her beauty. He presents her with a little rose in chased silver with six glistening rubies on the stalk instead of thorns.*

*   There is tumult on the staircase as excited voices, shouting and laughing, echo through the big house. The hall door is thrown open and the children burst in. They are choking with laughter and are out of breath, having raced each other upstairs. Their cheeks are glowing from the biting wind, the hot punch, and the fever of Christmas. There are four of them:* AMANDA, *the eldest, who in the autumn is to begin training as a ballet dancer in the capital;* ALEXANDER, *who is ten and imagines himself to be a martyr;* FANNY, *who is small, rosy,*

and resolute; and JENNY, *a passionate but withdrawn child, secretly in love with her older cousin* AMANDA.

The grown-ups now come in: EMILIE *and* ALMA, *embracing affectionately;* OSCAR, *holding the cheerful and sturdy* PETRA *by the arm and listening with a smile to his niece's chatter about some remarkable event at the domestic science school where she has been receiving instruction for the last two years; and last of all* GUSTAV ADOLF, *rather tipsy from all the toasts at the theater. He makes a risqué joke with the* EKDAHLS' *nursemaid, the plump and lame* MAJ. *She parries it with a giggle. From the kitchen entrance to the other apartment come the housemaids,* SIRI *and* BERTA, *and the cooks,* ALIDA *and* LISEN. *The professor's maid has gone home to Berlin for Christmas, an arrangement that suits everyone very well.*

Then they all pay their respects to HELENA. *The sons politely raise her hand to their lips, the daughters-in-law peck her cheek, the children give her a hug and a smacking kiss. Last of all the servants, who smile respectfully and drop a suitably deep curtsy.* CARL *plays a waltz on the piano.* GUSTAV ADOLF *inspects the dishes in the kitchen, and* OSCAR *tells his mother about the afternoon performance and the takings.* EMILIE *and* ALMA *drag in the heavy clothes basket with the Christmas presents and put it by the tree.* ISAK JACOBI *is noisily entertaining* JENNY *and* FANNY, *one on each knee.* ALEXANDER *and* AMANDA *have lost all dignity and are turning somersaults on the drawing room carpet.* VEGA *and* ESTER *bustle to and fro between kitchen, pantry, and kitchen, although everything has been prepared for several hours.*

LYDIA EKDAHL *is talking jabberwocky to* PETRA, *who cannot make out what her aunt is saying but who answers anything at all every time* LYDIA *pauses for breath.* SIRI, BERTA, *and* MAJ *have joined* ALIDA *and* LISEN, *and they are all whispering and giggling together. The topic is a favorite and inexhaustible one—* GUSTAV ADOLF EKDAHL's *avid interest in young women. All the girls have more or less truthful tales to tell of* MR. EKDAHL*'s philandering—both* MAJ *and* LISEN *can vouch for it at first hand. All the same, no one takes offense or finds his behavior improper. On the contrary, he is regarded as a fine upstanding man, well worth his distractions. Not even his wife can be bothered to be jealous.*

By tradition, Christmas dinner is eaten in HELENA*'s big kitchen, which is adorned with all kinds of Christmas decorations—runners, hangings, festoons, Santa Clauses, lanterns, and hand-dipped candles. By the same tradition, gentry and servants all have dinner together, sitting wherever they like. The food has been set out on the range and on the drainboards and the long serving table, which have been covered with gay cloths. Each one helps himself to his heart's content and his stomach's capacity. There is an abundant choice: countless varieties of pickled herring, sausages, headcheese, pâtés, galantines, au gratins, meatballs, steaks, and cutlets. To soothe the stomach and prepare it for further trials, a mild and aromatic puree is eaten. Then follows the Christmas ham with trimmings; and when the ham has been discussed and compared with the hams of earlier years, it is the turn of the stockfish, which is considered very wholesome. With the stockfish a white Bordeaux is drunk, which whets the appetite for a full-bodied Burgundy and a crisply roasted ptarmigan. On top of everything come the rice pudding, the stewed fruit, and the Christmas cake. Everyone talks at once, and nobody listens. Now and then one of the* EKDAHL *brothers gets to his feet and makes a speech in verse or strikes up a song.*

They drink vodka, beer, white wine, red wine, maderia, liquers, and brandy. They all shout each other down. It is only VEGA *and* ESTER *who sit stiffly in silence. They consider Christmas Eve to be the most trying day of the year. They consider it unseemly for servants to mix with gentry in this way. For more than forty years* VEGA *and* ESTER *have been compelled to endure this disgraceful meal, which, to make matters worse,* VEGA *has prepared with her own hands.*

PROFESSOR CARL EKDAHL *attracts* ALEXANDER*'s attention. He is red in the face and is sweating copiously; his blue* *eyes are bleary and slightly squinting behind the gold-rimmed pince-nez.* ALEXANDER *signals to* FANNY *and* JENNY, *who are rather tipsy from lemonade and Christmas excitement. The professor rises carefully from the table, excusing himself with a bow, and vanishes round the corner of the serving passage.* ALEXANDER, FANNY, *and* JENNY *sneak after him unnoticed, following close on* UNCLE CARL'*s heels with expectant faces. Now they have reached the hall.* PROFESSOR EKDAHL *has a lighted candle in each hand and he gives them to* FANNY *and* JENNY. *Soundlessly he opens the door to the wide, echoing staircase with ceiling paintings and sportive cupids, red carpets and brass fittings, marble-clad walls and window mosaics.*

UNCLE CARL *makes hushing movements. A trifle shyly he loosens his braces and unbuttons his trousers and underpants. The children's faces are pale with expectation.* PROFESSOR EKDAHL *bends forward, grasps the banisters, and grunts violently. As if by a miracle, a series of deep organ tones rise from* UNCLE CARL'*s fat bottom, ending in a clap of thunder.* FANNY *and* JENNY *hold their lighted candles close to the professor's behind. A moment of tension. Then loud gunfire booms through the* EKDAHLS' *staircase. The candle flames flicker and go out)*

III

While we are looking at the colorful picture of Christmas dinner in the Ekdahls' kitchen, I will tell you about the families' mutual attentiveness. They touch each other, shake each other, slap each other's backs, pat, fondle, and hug one another, give each other wet, smacking kisses, hold each other's hands, gaze into each other's eyes, and ruffle each other's hair. They enjoy dramatic squabbles, they burst into tears and abuse one another and seek allies, but they make it all up just as readily, uttering sacred vows and endearments. One thing is just as sincere as the other.

Despite the prevailing principles of upbringing, the children are drawn into the Ekdahl lovingness; they live as it were in a protective incubator of physical affection. Even Helena can show passionate devotion, particularly to the grandchildren. But even her sons and close friends are occasionally treated to the old lady's sensuous amiability. Toward her daughters-in-law, however, she is a trifle restrictive, grading her marks of affection in a subtle way.

They live in proximity, sharing joys and sorrows, quarreling and loving. The restaurant and the theater are natural outlets for the family's love of activity. They are unwilling to part even in the summer. The elder Oscar Ekdahl built four handsome country houses on a small headland in the outer archipelago. There, without starched collars and corsets, they enjoy the delights of the hot season in crumpled linen suits, billowing shifts, and wide-brimmed sun hats. The shady headland resounds to shouts and laughter, the flags slap in the breeze, somewhere a fiddle squeaks in an open window, a rake scrapes on the gravel path, a dog barks. The Ekdahls spend summer in Paradise.

(Christmas dinner is over, and now, singing, stamping, and sweating, the family, servants, and guests dance in single file through the rooms, holding hands. By tradition the dance is led by HELENA, *whose hair is coming down. One hand is clasping* FANNY; *with the other she has taken a firm grip of her wide skirts, revealing dainty ankles clad in silk stockings*

with woven flowers and butterflies. After FANNY *follows*
MAJ, *the nursemaid, singing and giggling, then comes* GUS-
TAV ADOLF, *his cheeks glistening with sweat. Under cover of
the general din he makes improper suggestions to the nursemaid. Following* GUSTAV ADOLF *is a long line of children,
who try to make as much noise as possible. Next are the
professor and his wife,* ESTER, VEGA, ALIDA, BERTA, SIRI, *and*
LISEN. *Then come* OSCAR EKDAHL, *who looks cheerful but
rather pale,* EMILIE, *and* ALMA. *In a loud voice, but with no
spite,* ALMA *remarks on her husband's flirtation with the
nursemaid. Next in line is* ISAK JACOBI, *who resigns himself
to the family's strenuous rites. Last of all the plump* PETRA,
*who is not singing because she has eaten too much. The dance
winds through both the apartments; the hall door and the
jib-door are wide open, the floors shake, the house trembles,
and the chandeliers tinkle. Laughing and puffing, they finally
sit down in* HELENA's *drawing room. The Christmas tree is
moved by careful hands from the bow window to the wide
doorway into the dining room.*

OSCAR EKDAHL *fetches the family Bible. He seats himself
on the raised part of the floor where the tree has stood. An air
of solemnity settles over the gathering.* OSCAR *takes out his
gold pen and opens the big book. The Christmas gospel is now
to be read, but first the year's most important events in the
family must be entered on one of the flyleaves, which are
already full of entries from previous years [ever since 1869
when the elder Oscar Ekdahl married the young actress*
HELENA MANDELBAUM].

*There is a quiet discussion as to what can be considered
important and unimportant.* FANNY, *supported by* JENNY,
*insists that the death of the cat Ajax is a sad event that should
be noted.* UNCLE CARL *appeals tactfully for the aged Aunt
Emma, who has also departed this life. Some regard Aunt
Emma's decease as more important than the cat's; others are
of the contrary opinion.* OSCAR *settles the dispute by jotting
down both)*

IV

(In the nursery all is chaos and excitement. JENNY *always spends Christmas night with her cousins.* AMANDA, *who has had a room of her own for more than a year, has dragged her mattress and bedclothes into the nursery to be with the other children. They have heaped their presents near the beds so as to have them handy first thing on Christmas morning. A pillow fight is now in progress;* MAJ, *too, has been drawn in. The children have long white nightshirts.* ALEXANDER'S, *which has red borders round the sleeves and neck, reaches only to his knees. They are all shouting at once.* MAJ, *who is rather tipsy, is yelling the loudest. A pillow splits, scattering a snowfall of tiny feathers.* AMANDA *seizes the chance to do the dance of the snowflakes, accompanying herself in a high falsetto. Chased by* MAJ, JENNY *rushes to and fro between the bathroom and the nursery. She screams for help.*

EMILIE *and* ALMA *come to say good night. Embarrassed and giggly,* MAJ *tries in vain to sweep up the feathers. It is decided to leave everything as it is until morning.* EMILIE *lights a small night lamp under a pink shade and puts it behind a three-paneled Christmas transparency, which is standing on the tall white chest of drawers. Then she switches off the electric light. The flame of the lamp blinks behind the holy pictures: To the left are the three wise men following the star; to the right the shepherds in the field hearkening to the angel's tidings; and in the middle Mary and Joseph, with the child in the manger, all drawn and painted with the greatest naturalness and wealth of color.*

It cannot be said that the EKDAHL *house is religious other than in a strictly conventional sense, but they say their evening prayers with the children, go to church when the bishop is preaching, and have vague ideas about a kind but remote God who arranges everything for the best, at any rate in the*

*long run. The children's prayers are fairly short and stereo-
typed; they say them in a loud voice in chorus, kneeling by
the bed with their hands clasped. "Thank you dear God for
this day, please make me a good girl [or boy]. Let the angel
be with me all night long. God bless Papa and Mama and
Grandpapa and Grandmamma, myself and my brothers and
sisters and cousins, uncles and aunts, Vega, Ester, Maj, Siri,
Berta, Alida, and Lisen, and Uncle Isak, and everybody else,
amen."*

*After the children have rattled off their prayers at top
speed, they leap into bed and are embraced and kissed by the
fragrant* EMILIE *and by* AUNT ALMA, *who smells of newly
baked bread. The good-night kisses and tucking in involve a
lengthy ritual, which is performed in a mixture of tradition
and improvisation. Then the two mothers withdraw hand in
hand, laughing and talking. From Grandmamma's apartment, music can be faintly heard. It is* AUNT LYDIA *singing,
accompanied by* OSCAR *on the grand piano. Suddenly all is
quiet in the nursery. The streetlamps cast rays of light on the
ceiling. The night lamp behind the transparency blinks, and
the figures almost come alive—it is as if they were moving
and whispering together.* JENNY *has put two fingers in her
mouth,* FANNY *presses her worn baby blanket to her cheek and
looks at the transparency through half-closed eyes;* ALEX-
ANDER *is lying on his stomach with his chin in his hands and
a battered brown teddy bear called Baloo beside him.* MAJ *at
one time made a suit for Baloo that seems to hold the lanky
lean body together; one ear is missing and his head wobbles.*
AMANDA *is sitting hunched up on her mattress with the quilt
over her shoulders, slowly turning the leaves of a large book,
which was one of her Christmas presents. On each page is a
prettily colored picture of a famous dancer or ballerina; the
text is in Russian. They are incredibly beautiful, and*
AMANDA *loves them passionately and longingly. A gust of
wind blows down the street. It moans in the tiled stove, where
the embers glow behind the round holes of the iron doors. They*

look like winking red eyes away in the dark corner. The wind, sighing through the tall trees in the town park, dies away and there is silence. Then, in Grandmamma's apartment, they all begin to sing. It has a sweet but sad sound.

Freut euch des Lebens
weil noch das Lämpchen glüht
pflücket die Rose eh' sie verblüht . . .

Suddenly the door to the nursery is thrown open. The electric light is switched on, and MAJ *bursts in. Her red hair is swept up into a thick bun. She is wearing an elegant bright blue evening dress, silk stockings, and high-heeled shoes. She stretches up her white arms and dances limpingly with twirls and hops, wild with joy)*

MAJ   Look at my Christmas present! Look what Mrs. Ekdahl gave me! I can't believe it! Aren't I *madly* beautiful? Aren't I beautiful? I look like a lady.

*(*MAJ *spins round, laughing. Then she puts the light out and throws her arms round* ALEXANDER*)*

MAJ *(Whispering)*   Tonight you can't sleep in Maj's bed because Maj will have a visitor, you see, and Maj can't have any number of men in her bed, can she now? All the same, you're Maj's sweetheart, you know that, don't you?

*(*ALEXANDER *responds coldly to her gushing endearments and lies flat on his stomach with his head to the wall.* MAJ *titters at her admirer's jealousy and tiptoes out.*

From Grandmamma's apartment comes the sound of talk and laughter. The grandfather clock strikes many strokes. It is answered at once by the cathedral and Trinity Church, which strike still more, first the quarters, then the hours. The air quivers and hums, now close at hand, now far away, as the wind plays with the sounds. Then all is quiet, strangely quiet.

ALEXANDER *is not sure whether he has slept for a while or not. Perhaps he has—the whole house is quiet, and so is the street.* JENNY *and his sisters are fast asleep, and the door to their parents' bedroom is closed.*

He feels that the moment has come. He cannot wait until next day—anyway it will be light then and conditions not so good. He gets cautiously out of bed, places Baloo on the pillow, and climbs over AMANDA, *who has fallen asleep with her book in her arms. The night lamp shines faintly behind the transparency, and the shadows move slowly across the walls and ceiling.* ALEXANDER *can clearly see the magic lantern standing on the big white gateleg table in the middle of the room. The lacquered tinplate is outlined against the pale bureau, the brass of the lens gleams.* ALEXANDER *feels a churning in the pit of his stomach. He shivers, but not because it is cold in the nursery—it is an ague deep inside his chest, almost out to the shoulder blades. He lays his hands on the marvelous apparatus. It is tall and narrow and ends in a small chimney. He opens a door in the box under the chimney and takes out a paraffin lamp. He lifts the glass off and strikes a match. A strong flame burns up on the wick; he replaces the glass and regulates the brightness, then pushes the lamp in and shuts the door. A pleasant smell of paraffin and hot tinplate spreads at once through the room. He turns the apparatus so that the lens is pointing to the pale wallpaper above his bed. There it is now, the magic circle. He adjusts a small screw on the lens, bringing the rim of the circle into sharp focus.* ALEXANDER'*s hands are shaking with excitement, he wants to wee-wee, and he is sweating at the neck. His heart is pounding loud enough to wake the whole house. Beside the magic lantern is a wooden box covered with blue cloth. On the lid is the picture of a family watching a performance with the magic lantern. All are in old-fashioned clothes, and the men have small pigtails with bows. The man working the lantern is a hideous figure with bulging eyes, big teeth, and a nasty, greedy grin on his fleshy lips. Beside him stands a fat woman in a red coat, grinding a barrel organ. The audience is upset, and a screaming child is being carried out to another room. The mother turns in the doorway and looks longingly at the stormy sea outlined on the wall.*

ALEXANDER has lifted the lid. The box contains a long row of glass slides, twenty at least. Carefully he extracts one and inserts it in the holder behind the lens. Immediately, on the wall above ALEXANDER's bed, we see a chamber with pillars and tall windows through which bright moonlight is shining on a white bed. A young woman is lying on it, stretched out gracefully)

ALEXANDER *(In a low, half-singing tone)* There she lies, the beautiful girl, the poor Arabella. Little does she know what awaits her. She is alone, alone in the whole house, oh, oh! Her mother is dead, and her father is carousing with loose companions. Oh! Oh! Oh!

(ALEXANDER's chanting has woken FANNY. She has tiptoed up and is standing close beside him, enraptured and frightened by the lovely picture and by his hollow tone.

The slide consists of two pieces of glass joined so that they can be moved independently. ALEXANDER holds the picture of the sleeping girl with one hand and slowly pushes forward the next one with the other. And behold the miracle! Floating on the moonbeams is an ethereal figure in a white floor-length robe. Her face is pale but has an unearthly beauty, and she is holding a wand that sparkles with starlight)

ALEXANDER Who comes there, as the clock strikes twelve in the castle tower? Dread seizes me. Oh! Oh! What is that terrifying white figure who is floating on the moonbeams and drawing near my bed? Oh! It is my dead mother! It is my mother's ghost. Have you come to . . .

(JENNY *wakes with a scream of terror.* ALEXANDER *just has time to lift the chimney, blow out the paraffin lamp, and dive into bed before the door opens and* EMILIE *appears in her nightgown and with flowing hair, not unlike the spirit in the picture. This scares* JENNY *into further howls.* AMANDA *wakes up grumbling.* FANNY *and* ALEXANDER *appear to be sound asleep. Sobbing,* JENNY *tries to explain that a ghost appeared on the wall above* ALEXANDER's *bed.* EMILIE *puts her arms round* JENNY *and assures her that there aren't any ghosts. She tells* JENNY *that she can sleep for the rest of the night with her. She picks up the child, who is still whimpering, and carries her into the bedroom. The door is closed, but* ALEXANDER *can hear his mother and father talking*)

EMILIE   There was a smell of paraffin in the nursery.

OSCAR *(Muttering sleepily)*   Paraffin?

EMILIE   Yes, there was a smell of paraffin.

OSCAR *(After a pause)*   There's no paraffin lamp in the nursery. *(Pause)* I'd better go and see what it is.

(*Grunts and groans. The bed creaks.* EMILIE *comforts* JENNY, *who has quieted down. The door opens and* OSCAR *enters, wearing a nightshirt, slippers, and a long green, shabby dressing gown that smells of tobacco smoke. He is holding a glass of wine*)

OSCAR   Yes, it does smell of paraffin.

(*He closes the door behind him*)

OSCAR *(Whispering)*   Are you asleep, you little brats?

(ALEXANDER *and* FANNY *at once sit up in bed, giggling expectantly.* AMANDA *turns in her sleep*)

OSCAR   What are you up to?

(OSCAR *pads about, then sits in a low nursery chair, sipping his wine and smacking his lips. He has had a little too much to drink and is in a good mood. Suddenly he gets up, grasps the chair he has been sitting on in his left hand, raises it on high, and displays it to the spectators*)

OSCAR   This is a chair, but not just any old chair. It may look like an ordinary wooden nursery chair, humble and rather battered, but you can't go by appearances. Because you see this is the most valuable chair in the world. It belongs to the emperor of China, and by strange paths it has found its way to the Ekdahl nursery. But watch, ladies and gentlemen, look carefully! Do you see the mysterious light radiating from the little chair? Yes, it's luminous. Just look at it shining in the dark! Now, my children, I ask you this: "Why is this chair luminous, why does it shine in the dark?" I'll tell you, but remember it's a secret and whoever gives it away is done for! Do you swear to keep silent?

ALEXANDER *and* FANNY   We swear.

OSCAR   Not so loud. Not so loud. Mama might hear us, and that would be the end of the performance.

(OSCAR *puts the little chair on the table beside the magic lantern and the other presents. He strokes it and takes a gulp of wine*)

OSCAR   This is the most precious chair in the world. It is made of a metal that is only to be found under the earth, fifty-nine thousand meters down, and only in China. It looks like diamond crystals but is much, much finer, more costly, more rare. The chair was made three thousand years ago by the emperor's jew-

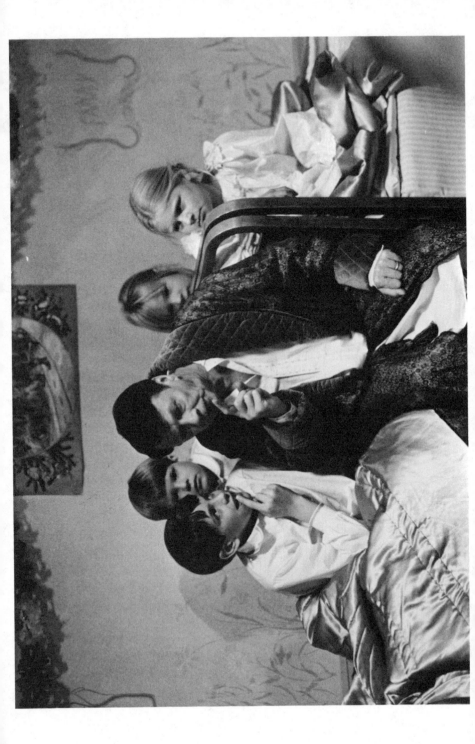

eler as a birthday present for the empress. She was very small, no bigger than Fanny, but she was the most beautiful woman in the world. She sat all her life on this chair. Wherever she went, she was accompanied by two servants, who carried the chair between them. When the empress died, she was buried sitting on this chair. For two thousand years she sat there in her burial chamber and the chair glistened in the dark, shining right through the empress's little figure. Then a band of robbers broke into the tomb, knocked over the empress, who immediately turned into dust, and stole the chair away. Now it belongs to you! It belongs to you, the most valuable chair in the world. Take care of it. It is very fragile and breaks easily. The metal, which has lived for billions of years fifty-nine thousand meters underground, has grown tired of the human race. It can crumble to dust just like the empress if you are not careful of it. Touch it gently, sit carefully, talk to it, and breathe on it at least twice a day.

(OSCAR *bows, his fingers on his lips, and tiptoes into the closet by* FANNY'*s bed. The chair is left standing on the table. It shines. In a few moments* OSCAR *reappears. He has pulled the dressing gown over his head and put on a villainous expression. He pads about the room, looking around him with wicked eyes, and stops in front of the chair on the table*)

OSCAR   What a damn stupid little chair! So battered and ridiculous! And more than a little ugly too.

(*He grabs it in his right hand; in his left hand he is still holding the wineglass, which is now nearly empty. He pretends to hurt himself on the chair*)

OSCAR   Ow! Ow! Devil take it! I think the confounded chair is trying to bite me. I'll give it what for!

(He begins to tug at the chair, trying to separate the back from the seat. He gets more and more furious)

FANNY   Don't do that to the chair!

(OSCAR stops at once and looks delightedly at his little daughter, who is standing up in bed looking angry. He puts the chair carefully down on the floor, sits on the sofa, reaches for the wineglass, and drains it. The bedroom door opens)

EMILIE   Are you all out of your senses? It's three o'clock already, and in two hours we must get up and go to early service.

(EMILIE tries to pull OSCAR up from the sofa, but instead he pulls her down onto his knees. She puts her arms round his neck, and he kisses her ear)

ALEXANDER   Can't we be in *Hamlet?*

EMILIE   Oh, I know quite well you've been talking to Uncle Landahl. But this is a matter for Papa and me to decide.

OSCAR   It's for mama to say.

EMILIE   It will be far too late for children who have to go to school next day.

FANNY   We can be pages in the first act.

EMILIE   If you're not in the last act, you can't be in the first act either.

ALEXANDER   But it can't be the same pages in the first and last acts because at least three years have passed.

AMANDA   I can be a page in the first act and a maid of honor in the last.

ALEXANDER   There aren't such small maids of honor even in Denmark.

AMANDA   The princesses were married off at the age of twelve in those days, so there could be small maids of honor too!

EMILIE   I don't want any arguing! Three pages in the first act on condition that you have done your homework and come straight home after the court scenes. And no grumbling about getting up next morning.

(AMANDA, FANNY, *and* ALEXANDER *declare themselves satisfied with such an arrangement, and their parents kiss them good night. As they are about to leave the room,* ALEXANDER *stands up in his bed*)

ALEXANDER   Tomorrow, and tomorrow, and
   tomorrow,
Creeps in this petty pace from day to day,
To the last syllable of recorded time;
And all our yesterdays have lighted fools
The way to dusty death. Out, out, brief candle!
Life's but a walking shadow, a poor player,
That struts and frets his hour upon the stage,
And then is heard no more. It is a tale
Told by an idiot, full of sound and fury,
Signifying nothing.

(*The audience applauds. The bedroom door is closed. For a few moments there is silence*)

FANNY   When did you learn that?

ALEXANDER   I know the part. I'm going to make my debut as Macbeth.

AMANDA   *You* are!

ALEXANDER   Yes, I am, see. (*Pause*) Flat-footed Pavlova.

V

(HELENA and ISAK JACOBI are sitting together on the sofa, seeing Christmas Day in. It has become a tradition, like so much else in the EKDAHL family. All the lamps have been put out, the candles in the tree have burnt down, the fire is crackling in the open fireplace, and a few small wall brackets of silver and rock crystal shed a gentle colored glow over the silent room. Helena has taken off all her finery and wrapped herself in a purple dressing gown and a gray woolen shawl. She has tucked her feet into large red slippers and plaited her hair in a thick pigtail. ISAK has taken off his frockcoat and draped a big soft blanket over his shoulders. His shoes are under a chair)

HELENA   There now, I've made some nice strong coffee, much better than Vega's awful dishwater. *(ISAK bows and murmurs his thanks)* What can the time be? Ten past three. We can sit for two hours, then I must change for early service. We're having coffee after church down with Gustav Adolf this year. You can go and have a nice nap, old Isak, but you mustn't forget dinner with Carl and Lydia. Last year you overslept. You said you had a cold, but you overslept. *(Sighs)* Oh, how good to have you here! You're a loyal friend. You're my best friend. Whatever would I do without you? *(ISAK takes her hand and pats it)* Last year I enjoyed Christmas; this year all I wanted to do was cry. I suppose I'm getting old. Do you think I've aged?

ISAK   You've grown older, yes.

HELENA   I was afraid so. I merely wanted to cry. Though I love having the grandchildren. I thought Oscar was looking poorly. He works too hard, he wears himself out with that wretched theater. And what's the idea of

his playing the Ghost? They could engage anyone at all for that part. He should spare himself. Besides, he's an awfully bad actor. I wonder whether Emilie realizes he is run down and needs to rest. I think I'll have a word with her. He's capable, of course, capable and conscientious. Just imagine, Isak, the theater pays its way and makes a small profit. Isn't that splendid! Not long ago I had to find at least fifty thousand out of my own pocket every year. Not that it mattered, but Oscar always felt so awkward about asking me for money, though he never spent it on himself. Carl does, on the other hand. He has now asked me for a new loan, but I refused. If he comes to you and wants to borrow, you must say no. Promise me, Isak!

ISAK *(Nodding absently)*   Yes, yes.

HELENA   I just can't make it out. Time and again I clear everything up for him, and after a year he's in fresh straits. He says he doesn't go to moneylenders, but I'm not so sure. Do you know?

ISAK   I know nothing.

HELENA   That awful German woman he's married to. She paints herself like a harlot. How *could* Carl have fallen for her?! It must be something erotic. What do you think, Isak?

ISAK   What did you say? Erotic. Oh yes. Yes, perhaps something of the kind.

HELENA *(taps him on the hand)*   You're not listening to what I say. *(Sips her brandy)* Never mind. The main thing is that you keep me company. *(Sighs, thinks for a long time, laughs)* Carl and Gustav Adolf are oversexed, they take after their father. He was oversexed. Not that I'm complaining, don't think that, Isak dear. *(*ISAK *makes a little gesture)* He was insatiable. At times I thought it was too much of a good thing, but I never refused. Gustav Adolf is hopeless. I've spoken to Alma and she says so wisely that she doesn't mind about his philandering, because he's the kindest and best husband in the world. It is fortunate that Alma is so understanding. Perhaps I ought to warn that little nursemaid—Maj or whatever her name is. She's very pretty, I must say, and good with the children. Bright colors, neat figure—pity she's lame, poor thing. But I won't interfere. What you don't poke your nose into you don't have to take it out of, Grandma always said. Are you asleep?

ISAK *(Waking with a start)* No.

HELENA Well, well. Carl and Gustav Adolf got too much and Oscar got nothing. What a tragedy for a passionate young woman. When Emilie was pregnant with Fanny she told me all about it. Poor girl! I must say she has handled her affairs in an extremely tactful manner. Oscar and Emilie are very fond of one another; it's a happy marriage in spite of everything.

ISAK . . . a happy marriage . . .

HELENA Are you sad because you have grown old, Isak?

ISAK No. It's just that it seems as if everything is getting worse. Worse weather, worse people, worse machines, worse wars. The boundaries are burst, and all the unspeakable things spread out and can never again be checked. It's good then to be dead.

HELENA You're an incorrigible old misanthrope, Isak. You always have been. I don't hold with you at all.

ISAK No, no, thank goodness for that.

HELENA   That doesn't stop me from weeping. Do you
take it amiss if I weep for a while? *(She tries to weep)* No,
upon my soul, I can't! Nothing comes of it. I'll have
to drink some more brandy.

(HELENA *sips her brandy. Suddenly she bursts out laughing.
She stretches and laughs*)

ISAK   What are you laughing at?

HELENA   I was thinking of Oscar—my husband, that is.
You and I were sitting here on the sofa, kissing madly.
You had unbuttoned my blouse—I think you'd unbuttoned your trousers too, I can't quite remember. Then
the curtain was drawn aside and there stood Oscar. It
was just like a farce by Feydeau. I screamed and you
made for the door. Oscar rushed off to get his pistol
with me clutching his leg. *(Laughs)* And so we became
friends for life.

ISAK   Your husband was a magnanimous man.

HELENA   *(Beginning to cry)*   Now, you see, I'm weeping.
The happy, splendid life is over, and the horrible,
dirty life is engulfing us. That's the way of it.

(ISAK JACOBI *draws* HELENA EKDAHL, *née Mandelbaum, to
him and puts his arms round her. He strokes her hair and
cheek lovingly, letting her have a good cry. It does not take
long*)

HELENA   No, my dear sir, this won't do at all. I shall
wash, repaint my face, do my hair, and put on my
stays and silk dress. A weepy, lovesick woman turns
into a self-possessed grandmother. We play our parts.
Some play them negligently; others play them with
great care. I am one of the latter.

ISAK   Good night, my lovely Helena.

HELENA   Oh, you were a sweet lover. You were like strawberries.

(ESTER *is standing in the doorway. It is hard to know how she came or how long she has stood there. She is dressed in black and newly starched. She bobs, her eyes lowered*)

ESTER   You wanted me to help you with your morning toilet, madam. The time is ten minutes to five.

VI

(*That same night* GUSTAV ADOLF EKDAHL *pays a visit to* MAJ, *the nursemaid, in her neat attic. He has brought a bottle of champagne. He is indulgent, lecherous, and rather tipsy. His clothing is in disorder: He is wearing a white starched shirt, undervest, long underpants, and black socks. He leans against the end of the bed, and the narrow, sagging bed complains.* MAJ *is sitting at the other end with her legs tucked beneath her. Her red pigtail is coming undone, and her nightgown reveals her pale freckled flesh. She is giggling*)

GUSTAV ADOLF   A coffee shop in Castle Street! Your own cakes and pastries and tarts and confections! What do you say to that, little Maj? Wouldn't you like that? You'd be the head of it, in charge of everything. Only yesterday I said to Alma: "Just look at little Maj, she's a princess." What breasts you have, my girl! No, no, I won't hurt you; let me see properly. Heavens, you drive me crazy! Now for a nice tumble. I'm a wonderful lover; all women say that. Here's both strength and tenderness. Let me see the little bush. Is it as fiery as your hair? Come to Uncle Gustav, little Red Riding Hood; I'm mad about you, my girl. I have been since the very first day you came. "I must have that girl," I thought. It was like a flash of lightning.

MAJ   Once you've got me on my back, sir, you'll forget all about the coffee shop. *(Giggles)*

GUSTAV ADOLF   I swear, Maj, my sweet. Wait a minute, give me something to write on. There's a pencil. Now I'll write: "Maja Kling is the manageress of my coffee shop, signed Gustav Adolf Ekdahl, Christmas night 1907." That's a contract, you see. Just stick it under a lawyer's nose if I should forget my promises.

MAJ   You must be careful, sir, not to get me pregnant.

(GUSTAV ADOLF *laughs and smothers the girl with caresses and smacking kisses. He grasps her leg and pulls her under him)*

GUSTAV ADOLF   You're no virgin, that's plain. Well, what do you say? Isn't Uncle Gustav nice? Have you ever seen such a crown prince, have you ever felt such a wooden leg? Not bad, eh? Whoops! Damnation! The rocket went off too soon. Oh well, can't be helped. Wasn't it lovely, eh?

MAJ   Oh sir, you're a real billy goat.

GUSTAV ADOLF   And you're my little lamb. Heavens above, I must lie on my back, I'm all of a sweat. I've eaten and drunk too much.

MAJ   You're not ill, are you, sir?

GUSTAV ADOLF   Not me! I couldn't feel better. Hahaha! How could I be ill when I'm with such a tasty little morsel. Sit astride me, my girl, and pop that obstinate fellow in where he belongs.

MAJ   Oh, you are a one, sir!

GUSTAV ADOLF   Now let's sing! "Ride a cock-horse to Banbury Cross, to see a fine lady on a white horse." What a glorious time we're having, eh! *(Laughs)*

(MAJ *lets out a howl.* GUSTAV ADOLF *puffs and groans. Suddenly the bed collapses and the ends of the bed fall on top of the lovers.* GUSTAV ADOLF *lets out a roar and lies as if dead.* MAJ *rests with outstretched arms and her hair spread over his face)*

MAJ   Lawks, how your heart's pounding!

GUSTAV ADOLF   I've a very good heart.

MAJ   Now you'll have to give me a new bed.

GUSTAV ADOLF   You shall have a coffee shop and an apartment and handsome furniture and a big bed.

MAJ   And pretty clothes.

GUSTAV ADOLF   No one will be more beautiful than you are. You'll be Gustav Adolf Ekdahl's mistress, and I'll come to see you every Wednesday and Saturday at three o'clock.

MAJ *(Laughing)*   How silly you are.

GUSTAV ADOLF   Eh?

MAJ   I said you're silly.

GUSTAV ADOLF   Silly, am I?

MAJ   Yes, you're a real numskull.

GUSTAV ADOLF   I'm not a numskull at all.

MAJ   Yes, you are, imagining I wanted anything from you.

GUSTAV ADOLF   Eh?

MAJ   Don't you see I was joking?

GUSTAV ADOLF   Joking? How?

MAJ   Now don't get angry.

GUSTAV ADOLF   I'm not angry, but I don't like being treated as an idiot. Stop laughing.

MAJ   I think you're so funny.

(GUSTAV ADOLF *makes no reply. He lies silent and with a set face. Then he sits up, climbs out of the broken bed, and puts on his underpants and trousers and vest and tailcoat. Suddenly he feels tired and sits down on the room's one rickety chair. His brow is beaded with sweat.* MAJ *tries to stroke his cheek, but he pushes her gently aside. She presses her palms together and stands there with her long flowing hair)*

GUSTAV ADOLF   I don't like being laughed at.

VII

(*The same night* PROFESSOR CARL EKDAHL *is overcome by a fit of depression. His wife,* LYDIA, *small and fat with slender shoulders, is sitting huddled on the bed, fighting tears and sleep, while the professor paces through the dark, tastelessly overfurnished rooms, wearing a dressing gown, nightcap, nightshirt, and slippers)*

CARL   It's as icy here as the North Pole. Why isn't there any heating? I can feel a cold coming on; my throat's sore when I swallow.

LYDIA   We have no credit with the wood merchant. We owe him a hundred and fifty kronor, *mein Carlchen; das weisst Du doch!*

CARL   To think you bloody well haven't learned the language in twenty-three years! Speak Swedish!

LYDIA   *Ja, mein* Carl. I make my best.

CARL   I *do* my best. *Do.*

LYDIA   Do. I do my best.

CARL   Last Tuesday I went to Mama and asked if I could borrow ten thousand to straighten out my affairs. She at once took out a paper that said I owed her thirty-seven thousand kronor. It's incredible.

LYDIA   You'll have to go to the Jew.

CARL   Thank you. I have already been. I pay forty-five percent interest, and if I'm not punctual he threatens to show the IOU to Mama.

LYDIA   I have some jewelry.

CARL   Idiot! Nice that would look! Professor Ekdahl running to the pawnbroker.

LYDIA   Aren't you coming to bed, *mein Schatz?*

CARL   It's hell. It's hell. I think I've a temperature. I'm shivering and sweating at the same time. This anguish. What's wrong with me? It would be better if I did away with myself.

LYDIA *(Weeping)*   You mustn't say that, *Carlchen*.

CARL   If only I knew why you paint your face like that. *(Coughs)* You look like a harlot.

LYDIA   When I *don't* use makeup, you scold me and say I look like an old crone.

CARL   Why did I marry you? You're ugly, poor, and barren. You couldn't even give me a child.

LYDIA   You never make love to me. You make love to all sorts of others instead. You're unfaithful. I know you're always being unfaithful to me, *mein Carlchen. Das ist die Wahrheit. Ich sage aber nichts. Ich schweige.*

CARL   Speak Swedish, Swedish, Swedish!

LYDIA   Poor Carl, how unhappy you are. If you weren't so upset and anxious, you wouldn't be so cruel.

CARL   The head of the faculty takes me to task and says I neglect my lectures. But I'm a scientist. I'm the only real scientist in this whole damned university. But nobody cares. The publishers didn't print my last paper. It was ill-founded, if you please. They only say that because I don't lick the other professors' boots. I feel ill. There was something wrong with the herring salad; it tasted stale. You can be sure the stingy old crone has been saving it since Easter. No one bloody well eats herring salad at Christmas. God, my head. I've a frightful headache. What am I to do? I must sleep. We have to go to that confounded early service too. Nothing but compulsion. Compulsion everywhere. And one must smile and be polite: "Dear Mama, how pretty you are today. You look like a young girl. Emilie dear, you've never played your Christmas angel so beautifully. How is it you succeed in everything you undertake,

Brother Oscar?" How do you do it? *(Wearily)* How do you do it?

LYDIA   Come, *Carlchen*. Come and sit by me.

CARL   You smell nasty. I don't know what it is. Have you given up washing, or are you starting to rot?

LYDIA   I don't smell nasty at all, *mein Carlchen*. It's you who have odorous hallucinations.

(CARL *sits down suddenly on the bed, draws a deep breath, and bites his nails, tearing off the skin near the cuticles. They start to bleed. He looks at the blood with satisfaction)*

LYDIA   Shall I bandage it up for you?

CARL   No, thank you.

LYDIA   Won't you try and get some sleep?

CARL   Yes.

LYDIA   I feel so sorry for you, *mein Carlchen*.

CARL   How is it one becomes second-rate, can you answer me that? How does the dust fall? When has one lost? First I'm a prince, the heir to the kingdom. Suddenly, before I know it, I am deposed. Death taps me on the shoulder. The room is cold and we can't pay for the wood. I'm ugly and unkind. And I'm unkindest to the one person who cares for me. You can never forgive me. I'm a shit and a rotter.

LYDIA   If you like, I'll make you a hot wine toddy.

CARL   Shut up for a moment. Don't be so damned servile. Wipe your mouth. Your lips are always wet; it's disgusting. I don't mean to be unkind.

LYDIA   I know that, *mein Carlchen*.

CARL   You ought to hate me.

LYDIA *(Shaking her head)*   I'm too good-natured, you
know that.

CARL   Oh, life! Oh, insomnia and odious bowels! Oh,
poverty and humiliation! Stretch out your hand and
you grope in a void. Why am I such a bloody coward?

*(CARL throws himself down on the pillows, the tears trickling
down his unshaven, bluish, swollen cheeks. Now and then a
dry, spasmodic sob rises from the professor's tormented breast.
LYDIA takes his hand and strokes it. He looks at her with
loathing)*

CARL   You have your amusements.

LYDIA No more now, *mein Liebling.*

CARL   The humiliations, the poverty, the bad food, the
icy cold, your damned ugliness. You swell and flour-
ish; nothing bothers you. I hit you and you kiss my
hand; I spit on you and you forgive me. You're repulsive. I can't stand your love any longer. I must leave
you. You can go back to Munich and we'll get a divorce. I want to be spared seeing you, smelling you,
hearing your damned jabberwocky, spared your
solicitude, your anxious eyes, spared your messy love.

LYDIA When you're depressed and upset, you always
talk like that. I don't take any notice of it any more.
You know that, *mein Carlchen.*

CARL   I want to sleep. Perhaps I'll dream of a sweet-
smelling female body, small breasts, narrow hips, long
legs. Fair-haired, cheerful, laughing. She puts her
arms and legs round me, pressing me to her. We copu-
late, her private parts are firm and generous. Oh, hell
on earth, prison, old age, disgust. Do you know why

I hate you so much, *mein Lämmerchen?* You are a reflection. Good nature reflects good nature. Mediocrity and ugliness reflect mediocrity and ugliness. I can see your poor face twitching, you have wrinkles round your mouth, you are grieving, but you put up with it. That's the big difference. I will never put up with it.

VIII

(At half-past four on Christmas morning GUSTAV ADOLF EKDAHL *comes down from the attic, where he has visited the nursemaid,* MAJ. *He has taken off his shoes in the hall and tries to move quietly, much against his nature.* ALMA *is already up, busy with her morning toilet.* PETRA *is standing in the middle of the room dressed in petticoat, stays, and curlers. She stares at her father and* ALMA *asks something from the depths of the closet. Getting no answer, she pops her head out and sees her husband standing in the doorway to the bedroom with his shoes in his hand)*

ALMA   Good morning, Gustav Adolf.

GUSTAV ADOLF   Good morning, Alma.

PETRA   Good morning, Papa.

GUSTAV ADOLF   Good morning, Petra.

ALMA   Petra, go to the kitchen and fry three eggs and some ham for Papa. Spread two cheese sandwiches. What will you drink?

GUSTAV ADOLF   Beer.

ALMA   You know where the beer crate is. No, wait, I think there's some stout in the icebox. You'd rather have stout, wouldn't you?

GUSTAV ADOLF   Yes, please.

ALMA   Hurry up, Petra. Don't stand there staring. We must be at Grandmamma's in an hour.

(PETRA *passes her father with downcast eyes and red cheeks.* GUSTAV ADOLF *attempts a kiss but she evades him. He sits on a chair*)

GUSTAV ADOLF   Give me some brandy, will you.

(ALMA *goes into the drawing room and fetches the desired drink. She hands him the glass, turns her back on him, and begins to put up her hair*)

ALMA   I have hung your clothes ready.

GUSTAV ADOLF (*Drinking*)   Thank you.

ALMA   There's hot water in the jug. I've just fetched it.

GUSTAV ADOLF   Thank you. That was kind of you.

ALMA   Hurry up, now.

GUSTAV ADOLF   Yes, sir.

(*He gets up heavily and begins to struggle out of his tailcoat.* ALMA *is sitting in front of the big mirror over the dressing table. Her bare white arms are raised as her hands busy themselves deftly with her thick hair, which has begun to turn gray.* GUSTAV ADOLF *is suddenly standing behind her. He puts his hands over her breasts and kisses the back of her neck*)

GUSTAV ADOLF   You're a damned handsome woman.

ALMA   And you're a big rotter.

GUSTAV ADOLF   Come on to the bed for a while.

ALMA   I've just done my hair.

GUSTAV ADOLF   Then we'll have a quick one standing up. That's not to be despised either.

ALMA   Petra will be here with the breakfast.

GUSTAV ADOLF   We'll lock the door then.

(ALMA *gives her husband a long look and smiles faintly. Then she gets up from the dressing table, goes out into the passage behind the bedroom, and can be heard telling* PETRA *to put the breakfast tray on the little table in the library. Then she comes in, locks the door, and takes off her long white knickers*)

ALMA   Come on then, but make it quick.

GUSTAV ADOLF   I don't think I can.

ALMA   What?

GUSTAV ADOLF   There must be something wrong.

ALMA   Gustav dear, you're not ill, are you?

GUSTAV ADOLF   Christ no, I'm as fit as a fiddle.

ALMA   Lie down on the bed.

GUSTAV ADOLF   Yes, I think I will.

(*He flings himself down on the conjugal bed, which sighs and sags.* ALMA *bends over him*)

ALMA   I'll bring the breakfast tray in.

GUSTAV ADOLF   Thank you, my dear.

ALMA   To think I haven't killed you.

(*He bursts out laughing and draws her to him. The big bed rocks and creaks. He gets on top of her and smiles triumphantly*)

GUSTAV ADOLF   Now what do you say?

(PETRA, *who has just put the breakfast tray in the library,
hears the familiar sounds from the bedroom. She makes a face
and involuntarily pulls her bodice over her breasts. The clock
in the dining room strikes half-past five. The first bell is rung
from the cathedral*)

IX

(*On the stroke of six and in complete silence the families
have early morning coffee in* HELENA'*s dining room.*
HELENA *inquires about the weather.* EMILIE *replies that it is
no doubt pretty cold.* VEGA *says her thermometer shows
twenty below zero.* ALEXANDER *yawns and is gently admonished by his father.* GUSTAV ADOLF *and* CARL *have a
dram of vodka, toasting each other stealthily as they know
that their mother disapproves of alcohol on Christmas morning.* JENNY *spills her cocoa and* MAJ *consoles her, saying it
doesn't matter.* PETRA *stares sulkily at her mother, who
smiles back and makes a resigned gesture as though admit-
ting that she must be crazy. Then there is a clatter from the
archway as the sleighs drive out from the yard, bells jingling and runners screeching against the cobblestones.* OSCAR
*looks at his watch and says it is time to go, and everyone
rises from the table.*

*They all pack themselves into the three big sleighs. In the
first sits* HELENA *in her sable coat together with* OSCAR *and*
EMILIE *and the children.* GUSTAV ADOLF, CARL, ALMA,
LYDIA, *and* PETRA *ride in the second, and the servants in the*

*third. The torches blaze, scattering sparks over the snow, and
the whips crack. The stars glitter in the still, frosty air. Dark
clumps of churchgoers, many of them holding torches, hurry
across the square, and sleighs of all kinds come from the
adjoining streets.*

The church bells are ringing)

I—A Death and a Funeral

Hamlet has been in rehearsal for some weeks and the
first night is fixed for the middle of January. This is
the first working day after the holidays and apart from
the usual colds and stomach ailments the little company is in good trim under Mr. Landahl's experienced
direction. The young and promising Mikael Bergman
is playing Hamlet. Claudius is Mr. Morsing, who is
rather long in the tooth, and Emilie Ekdahl is playing
Gertrude. Oscar Ekdahl, with a sigh of reluctance,
has undertaken the parts of the Ghost and the First
Player.

*(It is afternoon in the theater and they have been rehearsing
since nine o'clock in the morning. On stage are some flats, a
staircase, a bench, and a backdrop representing something
quite different from what it should.* HAMLET *and the* GHOST
are doing their scene. ALEXANDER *is lurking by the proscenium. Behind the concealing backdrop* EMILIE *and the
young* HANNA SCHWARTZ *have made themselves comfortable
together with the asthmatic* MRS. SINCLAIR *from the box
office.* EMILIE *is embroidering,* HANNA *is darning stockings,*

and MRS. SINCLAIR *is crocheting lace. On a stool is a tray with coffee and biscuits. Now and then they exchange a word in whispers.*

Round the walls—sitting, lying, or lounging—are most of the male members of the cast. They doze, yawn, scratch themselves, learn their lines, talk in an undertone, or watch the rehearsal, which drags on in the sleepy light from a single bulb hanging on a long cord from the flies.

HAMLET *is sitting on the bench, facing the auditorium. Behind him stands the* GHOST. *Down by the footlights crouch the* PROMPTER, *the* PROPERTY MANAGER, *and* MR. LANDAHL, *who is resting his head in his hands. He has closed his eyes; perhaps he is asleep)*

GHOST   My hour is almost come
When I to sulph'rous and tormenting flames
Must render up myself.

HAMLET   Alas, poor ghost!

GHOST   Pity me not, but lend thy serious hearing
To what I shall unfold.

HAMLET   Speak; I am bound to hear.

GHOST   So art thou to revenge, when thou shalt hear.

HAMLET   What?

GHOST   I am thy father's spirit,
Doom'd for a certain term to walk the night,
And, for the day, confin'd to fast in fires,
Till the foul crimes done in my days of nature
Are burnt and purg'd away. But that I am forbid
To tell the secrets of my prison-house,
I could a tale unfold whose lightest word

Would harrow up thy soul, freeze thy young blood,
Make thy two eyes like stars start from their spheres.
But this eternal blazon must not be
To ears of flesh and blood. List, list, O, list!
If thou didst ever thy dear father love——

HAMLET   O God!

GHOST   Revenge his foul and most unnatural murder.

HAMLET   Murder?

GHOST   Murder most foul, as in the best it is,
But this most foul,——*(Dries up)*

HAMLET *(Whispering)*   . . . strange, and unnatural.

GHOST   . . . strange, and unnatural.

HAMLET   Haste me to know't, that I, with wings as swift
As meditation, or the thoughts of love,
May sweep to my revenge.

GHOST   . . . Now, Hamlet, hear:
'Tis given out, that sleeping in my orchard,
A serpent stung me; so the whole ear of Denmark
Is by a forged process of my death
Rankly abus'd; but know, thou noble youth,
The serpent that——

PROMPTER   . . . that did sting thy father's life . . .

GHOST   . . . that did sting . . .

PROMPTER   . . . thy father's life . . .

GHOST . . . thy father's life

Now wears his crown.

HAMLET O my prophetic soul!

My uncle?

GHOST Ay, that incestuous, that adulterate beast,
With witchcraft of his wits, with traitorous gifts,——
O wicked wit and gifts that have the power
So to seduce!—won to his shameful lust
The will of my most seeming virtuous queen.
But soft! methinks I scent the morning air,
Brief let me be. Sleeping within my orchard,
My custom always of the afternoon,
Upon my secure hour thy uncle stole
With juice of cursed hebena in a vial,
And in the porches of my ears did pour
The leperous distillment, whose effect
Holds such an enmity with blood of man,
That swift as quicksilver it courses through
The natural gates and alleys of the body,
And with a sudden vigor it doth possess
And curd, like eager droppings into milk,
The thin and wholesome blood. So did it mine;
And a most instant tetter bark'd about,
Most lazar-like, with vile and loathsome crust,
All my smooth body.
Thus was I, sleeping, by a brother's hand
Of life, of crown, of queen, at once dispatch'd,
Cut off even in the blossoms of my sin,
Unhousel'd, disappointed, unanel'd,
No reck'ning made, but sent to my account
With all my imperfections on my head.
O, horrible! O, horrible! most horrible!
If thou hast nature in thee, bear it not,
Let not the royal bed of Denmark be

A couch for luxury and damned incest.
Adieu, adieu, adieu! . . . remember me.

(OSCAR EKDAHL *moves his arms and attempts to get up, but remains sitting with his face turned to* HAMLET. *He smiles uncertainly. His brow is beaded with sweat, the veins at his temples are swollen, he fumbles for a handkerchief and moistens his lips*)

OSCAR   I've forgotten what I am to do.

MIKAEL   You get up and exit upstage center.

OSCAR   Where am I?

MIKAEL   You're here. At the theater.

(OSCAR EKDAHL *seems to ponder* MIKAEL'*s words. He looks up at the flies and gives a sigh. The other actors realize that something ominous has happened. They collect on stage, silent and uncertain.* ALEXANDER *is still standing down by the proscenium, hidden by some painted flats. They all turn to* EMILIE, *who has left her handwork and her whispered conversation with* MRS. SINCLAIR. *She goes slowly up to her husband and sits beside him, stroking his head*)

EMILIE   Let's go home and rest.

OSCAR   Where am I?

EMILIE   You are with me.

OSCAR   What has happened?

EMILIE   You're a little tired, that's all.

OSCAR   What am I doing here?

EMILIE   You're rehearsing.

OSCAR (*Quietly*)   Rehearsing. Why was I rehearsing?

EMILIE   Come along, Oscar, and we'll go home.

OSCAR   Do you think it's a stroke?

EMILIE   We'll let Doctor Fürstenberg look at you.

OSCAR   Am I going to die?

EMILIE   Can't you help me a little?

(She says this to the bystanders, who at once bend over him and lift him up. His legs give way, but as he falls they manage to catch him under the arms and half-carry, half-drag him across the stage. The BUSINESS MANAGER *hurries down the sloping passage with the tall doors,* MRS. PALMGREN *immediately grasps the gravity of the situation and gets* OSCAR's *hat and coat, which they get him into with great difficulty. Then they carry him quickly across the square through the biting winter dusk)*

II

(It is a still day and the snow has been falling steadily. FANNY *and* ALEXANDER *have taken refuge with* VEGA *and* ESTER *in their neat room looking out on the elm trees in the yard and an iron gray winter sky. In here things are as usual; in the rest of the house it is all different. Everyone talks in whispers, doors are opened and shut soundlessly,* UNCLE CARL *and* UNCLE GUSTAV ADOLF *have called, their faces grave. Rehearsals at the theater have been canceled and* MISS SCHWARTZ, *her face streaming with tears, has hurried*

through the auditorium followed by a pale FILIP LANDAHL *dressed in black.* DR. FÜRSTENBERG *came early in the morning, disappeared for a few hours, and then returned. He is standing in the middle of the dining room having coffee.* EMILIE *has not dressed herself, although the time is already half-past one in the afternoon. She is wearing her long dark green dressing gown and her hair is plaited in a pigtail. She is quite calm and hardly ever leaves the bedroom and the invalid. When she meets the children she speaks to them in her ordinary tone of voice, but more gently. It is frightening.* HELENA *moves restlessly between the apartments; for once the jib-door is wide open. She speaks often on the telephone in a quavering, hoarse voice. It is unlike* HELENA. AMANDA *has been sent to school,* SIRI *and* ALIDA *are busy preparing the dinner; they do not speak to each other and do not clatter the pots and pans as they usually do. The nursemaid* MAJ *has shut herself in her little room in the attic.* FANNY, *who has listened outside her door, reports that she is crying all the time.*

Nothing is the same, but with VEGA *and* ESTER *all is as usual—here is a remnant of security.* FANNY *and* ALEX-ANDER *are sitting on* VEGA's *little sofa. They have an old, multicolored jigsaw puzzle between them. The elderly women in their dark blue dresses and blue-and-white-striped aprons are severely occupied.* VEGA *is ironing lace cuffs and* ESTER *is writing letters at an antiquated and fragile escritoire with a lot of drawers and pigeonholes. The two women talk in a murmur, without actually listening to each other. It is comforting, like the rippling of a brook. If they are grieving they do not show their sorrow, and come to that why should they grieve? In their old hearts they know that their much-loved* OSCAR *will soon enter into everlasting bliss)*

VEGA   I popped in to see the Gustavssons.

ESTER   —I'll just finish this letter.

VEGA   —and I met Mr. Albrektsson.

ESTER   Just imagine, children, this letter will go all the way to a little mission station in China!

VEGA   —and Mr. Albrektsson said his poodle had just had four puppies.

ESTER   A friend of mine lives there; she has been out there for fifty years.

VEGA   Mr. Albrektsson wondered whether Fanny and Alexander would like one of the puppies.

ALEXANDER   Mama won't allow us to have dogs or cats. She has told us once and for all.

ESTER   We could keep the puppy here.

FANNY   Could it live here?

VEGA   Otherwise it will have to be sold.

ESTER   When I was in China with my friend and we were doing field work, we had a dog and three cats.

FANNY   I won.

ALEXANDER   Shall we have another game?

FANNY   You take the red then.

VEGA   Mr. Albrektsson makes lots of money out of his pedigree dogs. But he wants to give the poodle pup away.

ESTER   He has a private income.

VEGA   It's his wife's money, my dear Ester.

ESTER   Do you really think so? I knew Mr. Albrektsson's father. He owned a large estate in the country and was anything but badly off.

VEGA   Would Fanny and Alexander like a treacle sandwich?

FANNY and ALEXANDER   Yes, please.

ESTER   There, the letter's finished. Fanny, you may lick
the envelope.

(VEGA *goes out into the kitchen and makes the sandwiches;*
FANNY *stands by the* escritoire *and pokes her tongue out.*
ALEXANDER *is suddenly overcome by unbearable grief. He
bends double and rests his head on his knees, his hands lying
limply on the plush of the sofa*)

ESTER   Would you like to borrow the flute, Alexander?

ALEXANDER   No, thank you.

ESTER   Here, you can lick the stamp.

ALEXANDER   No, thank you.

ESTER *(To Fanny)   You* lick the stamp then.

(*Quick footsteps are heard in the passage. There is a knock at
the door and* ESTER *calls "Come in!" It is* AMANDA, *wearing
a black-and-white checked dress, black stockings, and her hair
up. She is pale from repressed emotion but also filled with the
pleasurable solemnity of sorrow.* VEGA *puts the sandwiches on
a dish and turns round.* ESTER *stops pounding her stamps*)

AMANDA   Mama says Fanny and Alexander are to come
at once.

(ALEXANDER *shivers and his teeth chatter with fear.* FANNY
takes his hand and pushes him ahead of her. AMANDA *hurries
through the pantry, the long passage with the tall cupboards,
and the dining room. She opens the jib-door and leads the
other two through the smoking room with its oriental rugs,
ornate writing desk and bookshelves behind glass doors.*

EMILIE'*s workroom is called "Mama's little salon" and is
between the dining room and the bedroom. It is a bright room
with two large windows overlooking the town park, comfortable furniture, and beautiful pictures on the walls. There is
a baby grand piano in walnut in the corner by the right-hand
window, a low chaise longue by the end wall and an Empire*
escritoire *by the left window. An elegant rounded sofa and
small soft armchairs upholstered in a light-colored material,
an eighteenth-century chandelier, and a large carpet in a cool
pastel color complete the furnishings. The little room is full
of people, dressed in black and pale in the thin winter light.
All turn their faces to the children as they come in. There is*
UNCLE CARL *and* AUNT LYDIA, UNCLE GUSTAV ADOLF *and*
AUNT ALMA; *there is* MR. LANDAHL *and* MISS SCHWARTZ.
In one corner stands ISAK JACOBI, *his long bony hands clasped
on his stomach.* PETRA, *half-hidden by a curtain, is moaning.
A clock ticks haltingly. Voices can be heard from the bedroom.
The snow falls gently and incessantly on the big trees in the
park. The many people in the bright little room appear unreal, as though placed there like dolls in a dollhouse. The
bedroom door opens and* DR. FÜRSTENBERG *comes out. He is
about to say something to the gathering, but catching sight of
the children he checks himself, takes out a large white handkerchief, and blows his nose with a faint trumpeting.*

EMILIE *is standing in the doorway, still clad in a dressing
gown and with her hair in a pigtail. She beckons to the
children to come.* FANNY *and* AMANDA *obey at once, but*
ALEXANDER *stops in the middle of the floor. He is afraid. His
mother goes up to him, bends over him, and whispers something in his ear. He nods; she takes him by the hand and leads
him in to the dying man.*

*The light, painted blinds have been half-pulled down and
a soft twilight fills the room. The white-painted beds have
been pushed hastily together.* OSCAR EKDAHL *is propped up by
a mountain of pillows. The nightshirt gleams white against
his ashen face. He has closed his eyes. The eyelids are dark and*

swollen, his mouth is half-open, and his hands rest peacefully on the quilt. In an armchair with a high back sits HELENA. *She is suitably dressed, her hair and makeup are immaculate. An open book is in her lap. Her face is quite calm. As the children enter she smiles at them, holds out her hand, draws them to her one by one, and kisses them on the forehead—just as she always does. She immediately notices* ALEXANDER'*s terror and strokes his cheek briefly and tenderly.* EMILIE *has sat down on the edge of the bed and is looking fixedly at the sick man. She has taken his right hand in both of hers as if trying to warm it. On the bedside table are some brown bottles and a tumbler with a spoon.* OSCAR'*s pocket watch ticks eagerly in its little case. On the floor is an enamel bucket with a wet towel hanging over the edge. The clock on the chest of drawers says half-past eight; the pendulum is not moving. There is a pungent, sour smell that kills the mild scents from* EMILIE'*s dressing table.*

After a while OSCAR EKDAHL *begins to speak. He keeps his eyes shut. His voice is weak and rather slow, but otherwise he sounds as usual)*

OSCAR   You mustn't be anxious. This is nothing to worry about. I have no pain. Actually I feel better than I have done for a long time. Don't mind if I keep my eyes shut, the light seems rather glaring. (*Laughs*) I could play the Ghost now very well. Nothing, nothing separates me from you all, not now and not later. I know that quite clearly. I almost think I'll be closer to you now than when I lived. I want you to stand here facing me, one by one, so that I can see you.

(AMANDA *goes up to her father, who lifts his left hand to his forehead as if shading his eyes. He peers cautiously. His eyes hurt but he opens them and looks at his daughter and smiles at her)*

OSCAR   Now I'd like to look at Alexander.

ALEXANDER   No.

(ALEXANDER *presses his back against the door and shakes his head again and again.* HELENA *gets up, takes him by the hand, stands for a moment waiting, then pulls him gently over to his father, who grasps his hand and holds him fast.* OSCAR EKDAHL *closes his eyes and whispers something; his lips move but the words are inaudible. Then suddenly he looks intently at his son. It is too much for* ALEXANDER, *who flings himself down on the floor.* EMILIE *and* HELENA *lift him up; he is rigid with terror. They drag him over to the chair and he huddles up in it with his arms against his face.*

FANNY *shows complete presence of mind. She holds her father's hand and lets him look at her. Suddenly she bends over and kisses his cheek* ["*I'm three years younger than Alexander and wasn't afraid at all. I didn't even think it was disgusting, in spite of the smell.*"])

OSCAR   Tell Alexander there's nothing to be afraid of.

FANNY   (*Nodding vigorously*)   I'll tell him.

(EMILIE *resumes her place on the edge of the bed.* FANNY *and* AMANDA *sit on the floor by their mother's dressing table.* HELENA *is standing by the window and* ALEXANDER *is still huddled in the big chair. Now and then he peeps cautiously over at the dying man*)

OSCAR   You must take charge of the theater. Mr. Sandblad will make you *au fait* with the business side, and all artistic matters you will arrange yourself. (*Chuckles*) As usual.

EMILIE   I'll do my best.

OSCAR   A simple funeral, don't forget, Emilie! Nothing majestic in the cathedral with the band playing Chopin's "Funeral March" and the bishop giving a pompous oration by the bier. Promise me!

EMILIE   I promise.

OSCAR *(Softly)*   I rely on you but not on Mama. She'll want all the theatrical trimmings.

EMILIE   I shall speak to Aunt Helena.

OSCAR   Everything must go on as usual.

EMILIE *(Sadly)*   I promise.

OSCAR   I'll soon be dead. Will you hold my hand? *(*EMILIE *nods)* Eternity, Emilie! *(Pause)* Eternity!

III

(That night FANNY *and* ALEXANDER *sleep in the same bed. They have spent the evening with their cousins. They are all calm and composed and no one is crying.* GUSTAV ADOLF *embraces and kisses them and says that although he can never take their father's place he will do everything in his power to protect and help them as long as he lives.* AUNT ALMA *presses them to her soft bosom, declaring that from now on* FANNY *and* ALEXANDER *are her children just as much as* JENNY *and* PETRA. FANNY *retorts that she is still Mama's and Papa's girl and will never belong to anyone else.* ALEXANDER *says nothing and looks polite as usual.* ALMA *goes out into the kitchen and orders cocoa with whipped cream and apple cake for supper. Then they sit down at the dining table and play cards. Noise is heard from the floor above, thuds and heavy steps. After an hour or two* EMILIE *comes to collect her children. She*

is dressed in black and is very beautiful. She smiles all the time she is speaking; now and then she passes her hand across her face as though trying to brush away a cobweb. GUSTAV ADOLF, ALMA, *and the cousins say good night.* EMILIE *takes* FANNY *and* ALEXANDER *by the hand and leads them upstairs and into the dining room.*

The furniture has been moved against the wall and the big table has been carried out. In the middle of the floor stands the open coffin surrounded by lighted candles and flowers. OSCAR EKDAHL *is dressed in tailcoat and orders. He is very small, but neat, and has almost an air of satisfaction.*

FANNY *and* ALEXANDER *stand timidly regarding this strange and awful spectacle.* EMILIE *walks around, moving a vase or a candle. She keeps brushing her hand across her face.*

FANNY *and* ALEXANDER *sleep that night in the same bed. It happens sometimes—quite often, in fact—especially now that* AMANDA *has a room of her own. Nobody seems to mind.* AMANDA *sometimes teases* ALEXANDER *and says he's a sissy and should have been a girl, but as* ALEXANDER *never rises to the bait and* FANNY *says* AMANDA *looks silly with her huge breasts, the squabble peters out. Brother and sister go on sleeping together, unless they prefer to share the nursemaid's creaking, sagging bed. This is nicest of all, since* MAJ *is not only full of hair-raising true stories but also has a fresh, sweaty smell that is comforting.*

ALEXANDER *is suddenly wide awake. Grief stabs at him, but what woke him is a strange, far-off sound, a sobbing. He listens for a few moments and then wakes* FANNY. *This is rather difficult and calls for patience;* FANNY *is a deep sleeper and is always unwilling to wake up. At last the awful sound penetrates her hazy consciousness and she opens her eyes. Someone is crying.*

A sobbing, not quite human.

FANNY *and* ALEXANDER *get out of bed. The room is not dark—the pink night lamp is burning on the chest of drawers.*

*They open the door to their parents' bedroom. The reading
lamp on their mother's bedside table is alight. The room is
empty. The bed has been slept in and the pillows are on the
floor. Their father's bed is covered with a smooth bedspread.*

The weeping and the awful sobs can be heard more plainly.
FANNY *and* ALEXANDER *tiptoe to the dining room door,
which is ajar. They see their mother sitting on a chair by the
coffin. She is sobbing her heart out)*

IV

Oscar Ekdahl's last wish could not of course be carried
out. Funerals are for the living and not for the dead. The
bishop paid a visit of condolence. He is a handsome,
broad-shouldered man with a bony face above the gold
cross and the well-fitting cassock. He declared that he
himself wanted to read the funeral service over his
friend. What was the widow to answer to such an offer?
Then came the colonel in full-dress uniform with black
crepe round his arm and tears in the bulging bloodshot
eyes; he decided that the garrison was to turn out with
a guard of honor and that the band was to play Chopin's
"Funeral March." Emilie smiled wanly and made an
effort to look grateful, succeeding to such an extent that
the colonel kissed her hands over and over again and in
a voice thick with emotion assured her of his everlasting
protection and his deep respect. An hour later the chancellor of the university was standing on the drawing
room carpet, a very small man with great dignity and a

melodious voice. He was red in the face with agitation and said he represented not only the university but also the Students' Union, who wished to pay Oscar Ekdahl a last tribute. The beautiful widow, who is much taller than the chancellor, sank down on a chair and bowed her head. It was a touching sight and inspired the little man to discourse briefly on Oscar Ekdahl's pioneering achievements in the town's cultural life. On the same day the actors, with Mr. Landahl at the head, arrived in a body to take leave of their manager. Emilie offered them wine and cake, Filip Landahl read a short speech that he had written, and everyone wept openly. Emilie thanked her fellow actors and told them that on his deathbed Oscar Ekdahl had spoken to her about the future of the theater

EMILIE   An hour before he died he was conscious and quite clear in the head. He even laughed. We spoke of practical things, of the children's future and business matters. He also spoke of our theater. With great gravity he said: "Everything must go on as usual, Emilie." So we will carry on. At Oscar's request I will take over the management of the theater. Tomorrow rehearsals will be resumed. The first night of *Hamlet* will take place as already fixed.

FILIP LANDAHL *(Solemnly)*   In that manner we can best honor our manager, our dear Oscar Ekdahl.

After a short silence charged with emotion and broken by stifled sobs, the actors and actresses embraced their new managing director, kissed her, and promised diligence, endurance, loyalty, and talent. All quarrels and intrigues were forgotten. In fact life seemed fairly bright, cruel as it was.

Oscar Ekdahl's funeral thus turned out to be an event that overshadowed all else in the annals of the town.

(BISHOP VERGÉRUS delivers the oration, the garrison furnishes the guard of honor, the students form up in double line, the Freemasons' banners flap in the cutting wind, the military band plays Chopin, and the cathedral is packed with a respectful congregation, who are treated to a moving solo performance by MRS. HELENA EKDAHL, née Mandelbaum. In a few brief sentences charged with emotion she takes farewell of her son. They see the beautiful widow, numb with grief and leaning heavily on BISHOP VERGÉRUS's arm. They see the three fatherless children, who followed their mother, holding each other by the hand. There they are—AMANDA, FANNY, and ALEXANDER: AMANDA already prepared to take part in the ritual games of the grown-ups; the two younger ones exhausted by the overwhelming impressions of the last few days. The band plays, the organ booms, and the bells toll. The children gaze at their mother's long veil, BISHOP VERGÉRUS's huge back draped in the pleated cassock, and, up at the front, the gleaming brown coffin with silver fittings, raised on the actors' shoulders and rocking like a ship at sea. There are bumps and thuds on pews and floor as the congregation gets to their feet. Outside the opened doors the January snowstorm rages, and inside the cathedral it is bitterly cold, although the tall iron stoves are glowing. FANNY can hear her brother mumbling something to himself; it is mostly isolated words, one word for each step. She strains her ears, trying to shut out the noise and the funeral music)

ALEXANDER   Bloody bastard—pecker—shit—hell—cock —cunt—damnation—fuck—sod—stuff—bugger—arse —piss—prick . . .

(FANNY gives his hand a squeeze. He turns his head and looks at her gravely. She flashes a smile at him. Dusk is already falling as the coffin is lowered into the EKDAHL family grave. The snowstorm has died down but the air is bitterly cold.

The funeral dinner is HELENA's *concern, perfectly ar-
ranged and carried out. The many guests eat the fourteen
courses and drink the seven wines. The hum of voices, which
at first is subdued and tactful, rises during the evening to a
warm but dignified hilarity, drowning the string ensemble,
which from the drawing room is trying to create an atmosphere of bright melancholy.* EMILIE *leans to one side to listen
to* BISHOP VERGÉRUS. *His eyes are glistening and he never
stops talking.* EMILIE *now has a little color in her pale cheeks
and the soft mouth smiles briefly and modestly without disturbing the gentle gravity emanating from her slender figure.*

FANNY *and* ALEXANDER *have received their mother's per-
mission to leave the festivities and have retired to the nursery.
They are sad and sleepy and sit listlessly at the white table
with drawing paper and colored crayons. They are still in
their best clothes; the black woolen socks tickle, the sailor collar
is crooked, and the black bow in* FANNY's *hair is drooping.*

*From afar can be heard the buzz of voices from the dinner
and the mournful tones of the string band.* FANNY *yawns and
so does* ALEXANDER. *No one comes to put them to bed, to hear
them say their prayers, or to light the night lamp.* MAJ *is
helping with the waiting together with the other maids and
the waitresses from the theater restaurant.*

*Now the two children can hear faint music from the little
salon adjoining their parents' bedroom. A few hesitant notes
from the old, untuned spinet. They listen hard and their scalps
begin to tingle. Someone is in the little salon, someone is
playing Mama's spinet. Someone.*

*Without uttering a word they take each other's hand and
go through the dark bedroom to the little salon. A shaded
paraffin lamp is alight on their mother's* escritoire, *shedding
a warm, uncertain glow with many shadows and a deep,
yellowish darkness behind the furniture. A man is sitting at
the spinet with his back to the room and his head bent. His
hands feel their way slowly over the keys. He turns his face
to the children at the door. It is* OSCAR EKDAHL)

I—The Breaking-Up

(*Twelfth Night* *is being played. The performance is almost at an end and the last dance is over. All the actors have stopped in their movements, like dolls with eyes wide open in astonishment. All have had their wishes granted, Malvolio is brooding on revenge in the wings, and dusk is falling over the Illyrian sea. The machinist has produced real rain, which drips and patters against the windows of the palace.*

FESTE THE CLOWN [*played by* MR. LANDAHL] *has climbed up on a ladder and balances a lighted candle on his bald head*)

FESTE (*Singing to a lute*)   When that I was a little tiny boy,
With hey, ho, the wind and the rain,
A foolish thing was but a toy,
For the rain it raineth every day.

But when I came to man's estate,
With hey, ho, the wind and the rain,
'Gainst knaves and thieves men shut their gate,
For the rain it raineth every day.

But when I came, alas! to wive,
With hey, ho, the wind and the rain,
By swaggering could I never thrive,
For the rain it raineth every day.

But when I came unto my beds,
With hey, ho, the wind and the rain,
With toss-pots still had drunken heads,
For the rain it raineth every day.

A great while ago the world begun,
With hey, ho, the wind and the rain,
But that's all one, our play is done,
And we'll strive to please you every day.

(A moment's silence. Then there is a rattling in the tackle and counterweights up in the flies and the curtain falls. The audience applauds and the actors line up to take their calls. [EMILIE *plays* OLIVIA; MISS SCHWARTZ, VIOLA; ORSINO *is played by the theater's new leading man,* TOMAS GRAAL; MALVOLIO, *by the somewhat dissolute but very talented comedian,* JOHAN ARMFELDT; MARIA, *by the buxom* GRETE HOLM; *and* SIR TOBY BELCH, *by that pillar of the theater, the portly* MR. SALENIUS, *who wears a cloak and hints at secret vices.*]

The children are also in it, not only AMANDA, FANNY, *and* ALEXANDER *but also* JENNY, *who has managed to convince her mother that she is essential to the production. True, they wear the same page costumes as in* Hamlet, *but they carry trays with glasses of wine in the last act.*

When the applause has died down the actors gather around EMILIE, *sitting down on chairs that the stagehands have brought in or leaning against the balustrade behind* ORSINO'S *throne. The floats and battens are put out one by one, the rehearsal light is lowered, and shadows take possession of the stage. The gray light sways slowly and the actors' faces turn pallid and hollow-eyed. Some stagehands can be glimpsed in the wings, waiting to clear the stage as soon as possible. The safety curtain is lowered, rattling heavily)*

EMILIE   A year ago today my husband died. He wanted us to go on as usual, and we have gone on as usual, although everything has been different. We have had many successes and have played to full houses. We have been able to raise our salaries and to engage three new members of the company. We have kept together. . . .

(She breaks off and sits for a while deep in thought. When she begins to speak again it is with a different voice, almost inaudible and uncertain)

EMILIE   We draw the theater over our heads like a mantle of security. We hardly notice that the years are passing. That the sands of time are running out, isn't that what they say? The dressing rooms are bright and warm; the stage encloses us with kindly shadows. The playwrights tell us what to say and think. We laugh and cry and rage. People sit out there in the dark liking us; they are remarkably loyal although we often give them stones instead of bread. In order to justify ourselves to the world round us, we make out that our profession is difficult. It's a lie that the world accepts, since it is much more enjoyable to witness something hard than something easy. Mostly we play. We play because we enjoy it. If we don't enjoy it we sulk and blame the circumstances, never ourselves. So we pass our lives in a wonderful self-deception. We are sharp-sighted in regard to others, while glossing over our own faults. What about self-confidence, self-esteem, self-knowledge?—qualities that hardly exist in our profession. If someone says I'm good, then I *am* good and feel happy. If someone says I'm bad, then I *am* bad and feel miserable. What I really am I don't know, as I never bother to find out *the truth* about myself. All I bother about is myself, which is something quite different. I don't bother about reality either. It is colorless and uninteresting; it doesn't concern me. Wars and revolutions and epidemics and poverty and injustices and volcanic eruptions mean nothing to me unless in one way or another they affect the part I am just playing. There are actors who make out they take an interest in the world around them, but I know that they deceive themselves. I am not complaining or bemoaning my lot or making any accusations. But I am longing to get away from the world of the theater.

(The actors stand silent and dejected. No one speaks, protests, or argues. EMILIE *looks about her; she sees empty pale faces under the wigs and makeup, mournful or inquiring looks—* Is it me she's getting at? *She shakes her head as if the question had been asked aloud)*

EMILIE   You look at me as if I were angry with you. Quite the reverse. It's because we like each other that I dare to say what I feel. Perhaps I am really as selfish as I don't want to be. Perhaps I am wrong.

TOMAS   You have grown tired of the theater?

EMILIE   I think so.

TOMAS   Perhaps you want to leave it?

EMILIE   I think I want to leave it for good.

MISS SCHWARTZ   What will happen then?

EMILIE   Even if I do leave, everything will go on as before.

JOHAN   And who is to be our new managing director?

EMILIE   You must decide that yourselves when the day comes. *If* it comes. I haven't yet made up my mind. *(Pause, then with a smile)* And now I suggest that we wish each other good night. It's late and I have talked far too much. I didn't mean to worry you.

*(*EMILIE *nods to her colleagues, calls to the children, and withdraws to the dressing room that was formerly* OSCAR EKDAHL's *office. The actors remain standing on the stage, regarding each other shamefacedly and with tired, faint smiles)*

MR. SALENIUS   What I need is a drink and a sandwich.

TOMAS   I have had an offer from the Lindberg company, so it's all the same to me.

MISS SCHWARTZ   I think there's something behind it.

GRETE   Haven't you heard?

MISS SCHWARTZ   You surely don't mean it's true?

II

(It is a day at the beginning of May; spring has come and it is hot. Students and professors have pawned their winter coats and the girl students are wearing light dresses. The evenings are warm and there is an endless succession of festivities. At the theater they have taken out the Brussels carpet and the sofas and are playing a comedy by Scribe.

When ALEXANDER *comes home from school* AMANDA *and* FANNY *are sitting in the kitchen drinking cocoa and eating cheese sandwiches.* ALIDA *is baking fancy biscuits,* MAJ *is darning stockings, and* SIRI *is polishing copper.* ALEXANDER *senses at once that something is wrong.* AMANDA *and* FANNY *peep maliciously at him over their cups.* ALIDA *and* SIRI *do not return his greeting and* MAJ *looks upset as she hands him his cocoa.* ALEXANDER *immediately gets a pain in his tummy but says nothing.* AMANDA *whispers something to* FANNY, *who whispers to* AMANDA; *both giggle.*

Suddenly EMILIE *is standing in the doorway. She is beautifully dressed in a pale-gray gown with a wide, embroidered belt and transparent sleeves. She speaks to* ALEXANDER *in a serious tone)*

EMILIE   When you have finished your cocoa I want to speak to you.

(She turns and goes. ALEXANDER *sighs, puts down his cup, gets up from the table, and marches through the hall, the dining room, and the little salon. He knocks at the bedroom door; his mother calls, "Come in," and there he stands feeling ashamed without knowing why.*

 EMILIE *is sitting in the armchair by the window. The sun is streaming in over her; she is luminous in some way and not quite the mother he knows)*

EMILIE   We are going into the library to see someone who has come to see us. *(Pause)* It is someone who wishes to talk to you. *(Pause)* It's no good your starting to cry.

ALEXANDER   What have I done?

EMILIE   You know that best yourself. Come along now.

(She gets up and takes her son by the hand. They go to the library. There stands the bishop with a book in his hands. He turns round and smiles at them. From ALEXANDER's *perspective* EDVARD VERGÉRUS *is impressive: a tall, broad-shouldered man with a large bony face framed by silver hair and a beard. His eyes are a vivid blue. He is wearing a cassock and a gold cross flashes on the black cloth. He holds out a large hand to* ALEXANDER, *who bows from the waist.* EMILIE *sits down on the wide leather sofa)*

EDVARD   How do you do, Alexander.

ALEXANDER   How do you do, sir.

EDVARD   We have met before, you and I. *(Pause)* In sad circumstances. *(Pause)* When I officiated at your father's funeral.

ALEXANDER   Yes.

EDVARD   During the time that has elapsed since then your mother, for lack of a man to support her, has occasionally turned to me with her worries. That is quite natural. I am a close friend of your grandmother and am the parishioners' spiritual guide.

EMILIE   The bishop has been very good to me during this difficult time, Alexander, and I don't know how I should have borne it without his help.

EDVARD   We have also spoken of you, my little man.

(BISHOP VERGÉRUS *has seated himself by the library table and taken out a leather bag in which he keeps his pipe and a smaller bag with tobacco. He carefully fills his pipe and lights it, then leans back and observes* ALEXANDER *with his intensely blue eyes*)

EMILIE   I have told the bishop how proud I am of my well-behaved children.

EDVARD   You and your sisters are doing well at school, I have heard. You are diligent and attentive and got a good report at Christmas. Is that not so, Alexander?

ALEXANDER (*In a whisper*)   Yes, sir.

EDVARD   You mustn't be afraid. I am your friend and wish you well. You believe that, don't you?

ALEXANDER (*On the verge of tears*)   Yes.

EDVARD   Diligence and a good school report are not everything in this world.

EMILIE   Blow your nose, Alexander.

(ALEXANDER *blows his nose*)

EMILIE   Gracious me! How dirty your handkerchief is. Didn't Maj give you a clean one today?

ALEXANDER   Yes. (*Blows his nose, whispers*)   Damned shit.

EDVARD *(Ignoring it)* As I said, diligence and a good school report are not everything in this world.

EMILIE You must listen to what the bishop says, Alexander.

EDVARD Oh, he's listening all right, aren't you, Alexander? You're rather anxious to know what I'm going to say.

(ALEXANDER sniffles)

EDVARD You're a big boy now, Alexander. So I am going to talk to you as man to man. Can you tell me, can you describe to me what a lie is and what truth is? Can you?

(ALEXANDER has lost his tongue)

EDVARD You think that was a stupid question. It was too. I was only joking with you. Of course you know what a lie is and what truth is.

ALEXANDER Yes.

EDVARD Splendid, splendid, my boy. You know also why one lies. Why does one lie?

(ALEXANDER is silent)

EDVARD Why does one lie, Alexander? You must tell me why one lies.

ALEXANDER Because one doesn't want to tell the truth.

EDVARD *(Laughing)* That was a very sly answer, my young friend. But you don't wriggle out of it as easily as that. So I ask you, why does one not tell the truth?

ALEXANDER I don't know.

(ALEXANDER looks down at the floor. He can feel his skeleton leaving him and draining out through the soles of his feet and

spreading over the oriental carpet of the library. BISHOP VERGÉRUS *smiles to himself and pokes a long yellow finger into the bowl of his pipe to press the burning tobacco together.* EMILIE *regards her willful son with a sad face)*

EDVARD   We have plenty of time, Alexander, and I am so interested in your answer that I am prepared to sit here and wait indefinitely. You may not believe that, but it is true.

ALEXANDER   One lies to gain an advantage.

EDVARD   Well answered, my boy! Well and concisely. I now have another question and you must forgive me if I seem a trifle personal. Can you tell your mother and me why you have lied at school?

ALEXANDER   *(Staring at his mother)*   What?

EMILIE   Your form master has written to me and said that you have been spreading the most incredible lies in the class.

ALEXANDER   *(Beaten)*   What?

EMILIE   Will you deny that you—that you alleged to your classmates that—that I have sold you to a traveling circus *(Reading the letter)* and that at the end of term they are coming to get you. That you are to be trained as an acrobat and a circus rider together with a gypsy of the same age called Tamara.

(ALEXANDER *is silent)*

EDVARD   As you will realize, your mother was both horrified and upset when she read that letter. She didn't know what to do. I suggested that I should talk this unpleasant problem over with you, and here I am, as you see.

EMILIE   You should be grateful to the bishop for sparing you the time. You see, Alexander?

(ALEXANDER *bows his head*)

EDVARD   We are agreed that he who lies wants to gain an advantage with his lie. So I ask you quite logically: what advantage did you hope to gain by making out that your mother had sold you to a circus?

ALEXANDER   I don't know.

EDVARD   I think you know quite well, but you are ashamed to answer. You're ashamed, aren't you? That's good, my young friend. That's very good. It shows that you will be on your guard against similar fabrications in the future. Now you must ask your mother's forgiveness for all the sorrow and worry you have caused her. Go to your mother and ask her to forgive you. (*Pause*) You hear what I say, don't you, Alexander?

(ALEXANDER *has been standing with hunched shoulders and bowed head. His hands are clenched and he is no longer crying. He goes up to his mother*)

ALEXANDER   Please forgive me, Mama, for having lied, and I promise never to do it again.

(EMILIE *embraces the rigid* ALEXANDER *and draws him down into her lap. He sits there like a puppet that has lost its strings*)

EDVARD   There now, Alexander. The matter is cleared up and need never be mentioned again. Imagination is something splendid, a mighty force, a gift from God. It is held in trust for us by the great artists, writers, and musicians.

(BISHOP VERGÉRUS *has stood up. He repeatedly pats* ALEXANDER *on the back of the neck with his bony hand*)

EMILIE   I shall ask the girls to come in.

(ALEXANDER *suddenly notices that his mother is agitated and different. Her eyes glisten feverishly and she has red patches on her cheeks. She gets up with nervous vivacity and laughs as she looks at* BISHOP VERGÉRUS. *She hurries out into the dining room and calls to* FANNY *and* AMANDA. *For a few moments* BISHOP VERGÉRUS *and* ALEXANDER *are left together. Their eyes meet for the fraction of a second.* EDVARD *smiles, but* ALEXANDER *is stony-faced.*

Now they are all standing together in the library, bathed in the friendly sunlight: EMILIE *with the children, and* BISHOP VERGÉRUS *with his gold cross*)

EMILIE   I have something important to say to you.

(ALEXANDER *turns his head: Behind* EMILIE'*s back, half-hidden in the doorway, he sees* OSCAR EKDAHL, *who is regarding them gravely and knowingly. He takes his father's presence for granted; it is not at all ghostly.* ALEXANDER *wonders whether his sisters can see their father's presence as plainly and as close. Apparently not.* FANNY'*s attention is on a large fly that is buzzing against the windowpane and* AMANDA *is stretching her pretty ankle and peering under her long eyelashes at her pouting underlip.*

His mother has obviously said something and ALEXANDER *has not been listening. Or else* EMILIE *has dried up and for lack of a prompter has been struck dumb. Perhaps she senses the dead man's presence. In later years, when* ALEXANDER *had grown up and tried to recall that moment—his mother's face, the bishop's beard, and his sisters' movements—he imagined that his mother had perhaps been overcome by a sudden weariness or melancholy occasioned by the dead man's presence. At any rate* EMILIE'*s eyes are brimming with tears and she pulls out the little lace handkerchief that she always carries tucked into her sleeve*)

EDVARD   I am convinced that we shall—

EMILIE   Of course a great deal will be—

EDVARD   May God in his mercy take care of our little
family.

(ALEXANDER *seems to hear his father's gently ironic laughter,*
but the presence is no longer there. EMILIE *embraces her chil-*
dren and kisses them. She is weeping and wets their hair and
cheeks with her tears. Then she takes them by the hand, one
by one, and leads them up to BISHOP VERGÉRUS, *who bends*
down and kisses them on the forehead. He smells of tobacco
and mothballs)

EDVARD   I want us to kneel down and unite in a heartfelt
prayer. *(Kneels)* May God, our Father, in his mercy
take care of our little family and bless us and keep us
from all evil all the days of our life. Please, dear God,
give me strength to be a guardian and a worthy example to these fatherless little ones. Please give me
strength also to be a support to this lone young
woman.

ALEXANDER *(Quietly to himself)*   Piss-pot, fuck-pot, shit-
pot, sick-pot, cock-pot, cunt-pot, arse-pot, fart-pot . . . .

III

The bishop's palace lies opposite the cathedral and was
erected at the end of the fifteenth century. It is an elon-
gated stone building with countless dark rooms, thick
walls, tiny windows, high thresholds, and knotty

wooden floors. In the ceilings the beams are visible, and in the banquet hall and one or two other rooms they are painted with pictures from the Old Testament. Fires burn summer and winter in the old tiled stoves to keep the raw cold at bay. Below the west gable the river swirls past, black and deep; the wall pitches straight down into the dark water. The bishop lives on the top floor. The windows look out onto the street and onto a narrow cobblestoned yard. In the yard is a well, covered by an elaborate iron cupola. The rooms have old-fashioned furniture. The bishop and his predecessors have been indifferent to the comforts of life. The style is harsh and heavy. On the wall hang many generations of bishops and their wives, together with darkening pictures of holy persons with or without haloes. The bishop's book collection is housed in a room that goes through two floors. It is equipped with tall ladders and a balcony round the walls. Opposite the bishop's desk hangs a large picture of Abraham's sacrifice: The naked Isaac is already lying on the altar blindfolded. Abraham is holding the knife against his son's taut, backward-bent neck. An angel with a furious expression is approaching out of the clouds.

In the bishop's palace live three women. First and foremost the bishop's mother, old Mrs. Blenda Vergérus, a seemingly gentle and amiable lady with a superb carriage and clear-cut features. Henrietta Vergérus is the bishop's sister. She does the housekeeping and in every way is unlike her brother—small, dark, and lively, with piercing brown eyes and heavy black hair.

The bishop also has an aunt, Miss Elsa Bergius, who is enormously fat. She sits immobile in a chair surrounded and propped up by cushions and has hardly spoken for the last twenty years. Gossip has it that Miss Bergius was a beauty in her youth but that a shameful disease ruined her life. The kitchen is ruled by a ratlike shadow with a strident voice and skinny hands. Her name is Malla Tander and she terrorizes the housemaids and scullery maids, a filthy, stupid odd-job man, and a drunken coachman.

(EMILIE *and the children are visiting their future home for the first time and* BISHOP VERGÉRUS *is showing them over the house, followed by his mother and sister. They stroll from room to room and* EDVARD *speaks not without pride of his palace*)

EDVARD   In the fifteenth century, when this house was built, they didn't bother much about comfort. My predecessors were desirous of keeping everything just as it was, and I follow the tradition. Nothing may be changed or rebuilt. In these old rooms there is a beauty that is imperishable. Let us be grateful that we are allowed to live in an atmosphere of purity and austerity.

(*It should be pointed out that* BISHOP VERGÉRUS *states his views with polite amiability. He speaks with sincerity and warmth and keeps his arm protectively round* EMILIE*'s shoulders* [*pressing her imperceptibly to him*]. *He is holding* FANNY *by the hand.* AMANDA *and* ALEXANDER *bring up the rear dejectedly. The bishop's mother and sister,* BLENDA *and* HENRIETTA VERGÉRUS, *hurry ahead, smiling and obliging. In various ways the two women try to show* EMILIE *that she is welcome, that their dear son and brother has made a good choice*)

EDVARD   I want you to meet my aunt. Don't be alarmed, Emilie. Don't be afraid, children, it's quite all right. Now you can open the door, sister dear. This is my aunt, Miss Elsa Bergius. Good afternoon, Aunt. How are you today? Just imagine, we have a visitor, and not just any visitor. It is my future wife! Emilie Ekdahl,

the famous actress, whom you are sure to have heard
of.

EMILIE   How do you do, Miss Bergius. Come and say
how do you do nicely to Aunt Bergius, children. Come
along, Amanda, don't hang back like that.

EDVARD   No, no, it doesn't matter. If Fanny and Alexander don't want to say how do you do today, they can
do it some other time. It doesn't matter in the least. We
won't force them.

*(The shapeless woman regards the children with sharp eyes
behind the eyelids' rolls of fat. She gives a faint, sarcastic
smile and nods several times. When she breathes she lets out
a sound like that of a rusty pump. A smell of sour dampness
surrounds the sunken figure)*

EDVARD   And now it is time to meet Mrs. Tander, our
capable cook, who has lived with our family for thirty
years. Good afternoon, Mrs. Tander. This is my future wife, Mrs. Emilie Ekdahl, and these are her children, Amanda, Fanny, and Alexander.

MRS. TANDER *(Bobbing)*   How do you do, Mrs. Ekdahl.

EMILIE *(Horrified)*   How do you do, Mrs. Tander.

HENRIETTA   And these are our capable helpers, Karna,
Selma, and little Justine. The odd-job man you will
meet another time, he has gone on an errand, and the
coachman is sick, as usual. Shall we have dinner?

*(They all return to the upper regions. The mighty stone stair-
case with the tall pillars and the narrow, green-glassed
windows echoes with voices and forced laughter.* BISHOP
VERGÉRUS *has taken* EMILIE *by the hand and drawn her into
the bedroom. They are both slightly out of breath, having
hurried ahead of the others)*

EDVARD   I have a wish. A single wish, but an important one. I want to tell you my wish immediately so that you will have a chance of changing your mind if you consider it impossible to comply with.

EMILIE   Tell me your wish.

EDVARD   I want you and your children to come to my house without possessions.

EMILIE   What do you mean?

EDVARD   You are a wealthy woman. You are used to a luxury that I cannot give you. So I want you to leave the theater.

EMILIE   We have already agreed about that. Kiss me now and say that I am God's gift to the bishop.

EDVARD *(Kissing her quickly)*   I want you to leave your home, your clothes, your jewels, your furniture, your friends, your possessions, your habits, your thoughts. I want you to leave your former life entirely.

EMILIE   Am I to come naked?

EDVARD *(Smiling)*   I am serious, my darling. You are to come to your new life as though newly born.

EMILIE   And the children?

EDVARD   The children too.

EMILIE   Their toys, their dolls, books, small . . .

EDVARD *(Breaking in)*   Nothing.

EMILIE   I must talk to the children.

EDVARD   It is for you to decide, Emilie.

EMILIE   I can decide for my own part. Not for the children. That's why I must ask them.

EDVARD They must sacrifice something for their mother's happiness.

EMILIE You are angry already. Kiss me!

EDVARD I am not in the least angry. *(Smiles and kisses her)*

EMILIE I'll win them over all right.

EDVARD You must think carefully, Emilie.

EMILIE I have already thought. My life has been empty and superficial, thoughtless and comfortable. I have always longed for the life you live.

EDVARD I know, I know.

EMILIE For me it is not hard to grant your wish. I do so with joy.

EDVARD *(With tears in his eyes)* I want us to live close to each other. We shall live before the face of God.

EMILIE I shall learn to understand what you mean when you say that we shall live before the face of God.

EDVARD I have told you how my wife and my two children lost their lives down there in the river fifteen years ago. For many years I dragged myself through life like a gray earthworm. I saw you in the distance, always together with other people. You were inaccessible, but I waited for you. My longing and my waiting became the best part of my life. Now I have my arms round you and you have promised to come to me for always. It is an incomprehensible grace.

EMILIE I'm afraid I have never concerned myself for anything in life. Not my profession or my children or any single human being. Sometimes I have wondered whether there was something radically wrong with my feelings. I could not understand why nothing re-

ally hurt, why I never felt really happy. Now I know
that the crucial moment is here. I know that we shall
pain each other; I know it but I am not afraid. I know
too that we shall make each other happy and I weep
with fear because the time is so short, the days pass so
quickly, nothing lasts for ever. You say that your God
is the God of love. It sounds so beautiful and I wish
I could believe as you do. Perhaps I will one day. My
God is different, Edvard. He is like myself, fluid and
boundless and intangible, both in his cruelty and his
tenderness. I am an actress; I am used to wearing
masks. My God wears a thousand masks. He has never
shown me his real face, just as I am incapable of showing you or God my real face. Through you I shall learn
to know God's being. Kiss me now and hold me in
your arms, quite still, as only you can, my darling.

IV

(The wedding takes place on a bright early summer's day in
HELENA's *large drawing room. It is conducted by* BISHOP
VERGÉRUS's *uncle,* AN ANCIENT CLERGYMAN *from the plain.*
It has been decided that only family and close friends are to
be present, but it is a large gathering nevertheless: GUSTAV
ADOLF *and* ALMA *with their children,* PETRA *and* JENNY;
CARL *and* LYDIA; ISAK JACOBI; *and several of the actors from*
the theater—FILIP LANDAHL, *little* MISS SCHWARTZ, *the*
handsome TOMAS GRAAL, *and* GRETE HOLM. *From the*
BISHOP's *side come his mother and his sister* HENRIETTA.

ESTER, VEGA *and the ratlike* MALLA TANDER *are also in a prominent position. The rest of the servants crowd in the doorway.*

At the BISHOP*'s request the ladies wear simple dark dresses, the two clergymen their clerical garbs, and the other men tailcoats. The impression is perhaps one of a mourning ceremony.*

The bride is composed but pale. The groom is overwhelmed from time to time by emotion and has to keep blowing his nose. AMANDA *and* FANNY *are reveling in the romantic aspect of the situation, without a thought for what lies ahead of them.* ALEXANDER *is ill and has a temperature, but is thought to be fit enough to be present. His eyes are wide open and his mouth gapes with astonishment: In the sunlight just behind the statue of Venus de Milo stands* OSCAR EKDAHL, *following the ceremony with smiling interest.*

When all is over there are a few moments of relief. The EKDAHLS' *fondness for embracing breaks all barriers: They kiss each other, gaze into each other's eyes, shed real tears, and press each other's hands. The* BISHOP *suddenly feels included in a family fellowship, which moves and bewilders him. The champagne is brought in, toasts are made to right and left, and the atmosphere eases and becomes almost gay.* FILIP LANDAHL *feels called upon to make a speech, although all speeches are banned, a fact he mentions at the outset while assuring everyone that what he is going to say is not a speech at all but an outburst of affection for his dear* EMILIE EKDAHL, *the great actress and wonderful person. He thanks her for the time that has been and expresses a hope that she will soon be standing on the stage again, surrounded by her fellow actors. Here* FILIP LANDAHL *waxes biblical and quotes the Master's words about the light and the bushel, after which, enlivened by three glasses of champagne, he declares that the theater is just as good a church as the cathedral and that all actors and bishops and musicians and vicars and painters and curates are one single clergy, whose duty it is, each in his own church, to serve the living God. Deeply moved by his own words the old actor goes up to the bride and gives her a smacking kiss on the lips, after which he shakes the groom's hand in both of his and [being the elder] suggests that they call each other by their Christian names.* BISHOP VERGÉRUS *not at all pleased by such presumption, gives a forced smile and says his name is Edvard.* FILIP LANDAHL *slaps him on the shoulder and roars with laughter as though it were all a capital joke.*

Farewells are now made. At BISHOP VERGÉRUS*'s request the new family, taking no possessions with them, is to walk the short distance from the* EKDAHLS' *house in the square to the bishop's palace. When all the good-byes have been said in a tumult of feelings, they set off on foot for their new home:* EDVARD VERGÉRUS, *with his wife* EMILIE *on his arm and the three children trailing behind.* EMILIE, *filled with her shining hopes of a new life, radiates strength and confidence.* BISHOP VERGÉRUS, *proud of his beautiful wife, bows to right and left, raising his pleated doctor's hat to those he meets. The general opinion is that art and religion have formed a happy union. On the other hand, no one comments on the three children, who bring up the rear.*

The EKDAHLS *stand in the windows of* HELENA*'s drawing room, watching the strange departure from behind concealing curtains. The temporary emotional storm has died down and the champagne has worn off. They all have a sudden and violent sense of loss)*

ALMA   I wonder if this is a good thing.

LYDIA   You saw how happy she was, dear Emilie.

HELENA   I'm thinking of the children.

GUSTAV ADOLF   They'll get used to it, Mama dear.

CARL   They say he's the devil of a lady-killer, the bishop.

LYDIA   I'm sure that's just gossip, *mein Carlchen.*

ALMA   I don't know why, I just want to cry.

HELENA   I do think they might have treated themselves to a honeymoon.

GUSTAV ADOLF   I wanted to invite them to our house in Provence, but Emilie wouldn't let me.

ALMA   She has a terrible respect for her new husband.

LYDIA   A handsome man, say what you like.

PETRA *(Suddenly)*   He has false teeth.

ALMA   I never heard anything so silly. He hasn't.

HELENA   His mother was charming.

CARL   But the sister is said to be a hell of a virago.

GUSTAV ADOLF   And that cook looked like a sewer rat.

HELENA *(Unhappily)*   I think we'll have Emilie back. Quite soon.

V

(In the bishop's palace they are having supper. A fire is burning in the open fireplace, fighting a losing battle with the chill dampness that rises from the darkness of the river. The setting sun throws bright rays through the gloomy room.

For the first time they are sitting together at the heavy oak table: BISHOP VERGÉRUS *and* EMILIE *at either end, the children along one side,* BLENDA *and* HENRIETTA *on the other.*

Between them they have the shapeless MISS BERGIUS, *whom they take it in turns to feed. The fat woman whimpers. When she slowly chews with her toothless gums she closes her eyes and a barely audible growl rises from her throat. Two shadowy creatures with gray faces and downcast eyes do the waiting. They are* SELMA *and* JUSTINE. *There is no sign of* MALLA TANDER)

EDVARD *(Cheerfully)* Well, here we are at table for the first time.

HENRIETTA The children don't seem to have any appetite.

EMILIE You must understand, Henrietta, that they are disquietened by their new and strange surroundings. It's only natural.

HENRIETTA It could also be that they are turning up their noses at the good bread and the tasty food.

EDVARD This evening let us be glad, Henrietta.

HENRIETTA I have no desire to spoil our first evening together with severity, but in future (it is just as well for me to mention it at once) in future no one will be allowed to leave the table without having eaten up everything on . . .

EMILIE *(Breaking in)* Henrietta dear, *I* am the one to tell my children what to do. It is for me to say . . .

HENRIETTA *(Interrupting)* There is a fundamental rule in this house that no one must break, not even you, Emilie dear, and that is respect for the temporal gifts.

EMILIE I think you have misunderstood something essential, dearest Henrietta, but I suggest we postpone this discussion until a more suitable opportunity.

HENRIETTA   Forgive me, Emilie dear. I am forgetting myself. Forgive me!

EMILIE   I am sure you are a much more capable housewife than I am. I shall ask your advice in all things.

HENRIETTA   Edvard has admonished me a hundred times. *(Weeps and laughs)* It is not easy, let me tell you. *(Pause)* It is not easy to realize that one has become superfluous.

BLENDA   That will do, Henrietta.

(HENRIETTA *stops crying at once and gives her mother a strange, timid look.* MISS BERGIUS*'s throat growls faintly. The children sulk over their plates, which are filled to the brim with gruel)*

HENRIETTA *(Smiling)*   Something that I perhaps may *be allowed* to say is that we are early risers in this house, both on weekdays and Sundays. At six o'clock we gather for morning prayers in Edvard's study. I should also like to mention that we make our own beds and tidy our rooms ourselves. In this house punctuality, cleanliness, and order are the rule.

BLENDA   Don't be alarmed, children. My daughter does not mean to be as strict as she may sound. At first we will take everything lightly.

EMILIE   I don't quite see what you mean, Blenda. If the intention is to introduce some new method of upbringing . . .

BLENDA *(Interrupting)*   Not at all, Emilie dear! Not at all! I am sure the children themselves will gradually realize how pleasant it is to perform one's duties conscientiously. I mean it is all to be like a game.

EMILIE   I don't think my children care for that sort of game. Nor do I, come to that.

BLENDA   Time will show, my dear Emilie.

EDVARD *(Mediating)*   Let us now clasp our hands and say grace. Thank you, O God, for what we have received this day, and for giving us the necessities of life. May we, with generous hearts, share our abundance with those who hunger and thirst. Amen.

ALEXANDER *(Softly)*   Cock—cunt—arse-hole—piss—shit —bloody, fucking hell . . .

(FANNY *giggles.* AMANDA *hushes her*)

EDVARD   And what have you to say that is so amusing, Alexander?

(ALEXANDER *makes no reply, but turns red in the face.* FANNY*'s giggles get worse.* AMANDA *shakes her head and has a drink of water to stifle her laughter*)

EDVARD   Let me tell you, my dear Alexander, that your stepfather has excellent hearing—I might almost say that his ears are frighteningly sharp. Shall we rise from the table? In an hour we shall meet in the library for a little reading aloud and handwork. Henrietta, perhaps you would kindly show the children where they are to sleep.

VI

(*The children's rooms are freshly painted, wallpapered, and scrubbed. They open onto the narrow cobblestoned yard with the deep well. A large room has been partitioned off;* FANNY *and* AMANDA *have been given the bigger half and* ALEX-ANDER *the triangular part that is left. The cots are brown-stained with wooden bars and hard mattresses, and the sheets are coarse and damp. The furnishings are sparse. An old-fashioned and ingeniously planned doll's house stands against the wall. A low table and one or two clumsy nursery chairs are by the window. In* ALEXANDER's *room there is a bookcase filled with illustrated books in foreign languages and tattered old weekly magazines. On the walls hang pictures with biblical themes: The Infant Jesus stands among tame and wild animals with a palm leaf in his hand. He is smiling insipidly. Another picture shows an angel with seven gilded candles hovering over a sleeping house in a wintry landscape. We can also see Pharaoh's daughter leaning over a basket that is floating among the bulrushes. In the basket lies a fat baby as pink as a pig. The blinds are painted with vines and tall castles. The floorboards are knotty and splintery and have no mats. In one corner is a broken old rocking horse with a spiteful expression. A flute is lying on a shelf.*

When the children have washed in the icy water and gotten into bed under the supervision of the skinny JUSTINE, *their mother and stepfather come to say goodnight. The regular prayers are said in unison.* UNCLE EDVARD *is added to the string of persons who are to be enfolded by God's special care: God bless Papa and Mama, Grandpa and Uncle Edvard, etc.* ALEXANDER *says his personal variant, changing the bishop into Piss-pot, and refuses to kiss both his mother and his stepfather. In return* BISHOP VERGÉRUS *gives him a caress that is more like a box on the ears.* ALEXANDER *chokes back the lump in his throat and pokes his tongue out at the bishop's black back.* EMILIE *asks her husband to go ahead to the bedroom. He hesitates but complies. He turns round in the doorway and the light in the outer room gives his figure terrifying proportions)*

EDVARD   My dearest wish is to live at peace with each
other. Love cannot be commanded, but we can show
one another respect and consideration.

*(He says this in a low, toneless voice, sorrowfully. As no one
answers he nods curtly and withdraws, his footsteps on the
flagstones echoing in the high passage leading to the bedroom)*

AMANDA   Whose is that doll's house?

EMILIE *(Gently)*   Fifteen years ago two little girls lived in
this room.

AMANDA   They were drowned, weren't they?

ALEXANDER   Their mother too.

FANNY   Perhaps the house is haunted!

EMILIE   Don't be silly now, Fanny. There are no such
things as ghosts.

AMANDA   Did the children really live in this room?

EMILIE   Yes, I think this was the nursery.

FANNY   One day when it's getting dark and I come into
this room there will be two pale little girls dressed in
black in front of the doll's house and they'll say in a
whisper that they've come to play with me.

EMILIE   *(Laughing)*   Quiet now, Fanny. Don't be ridiculous!

FANNY   Then they'll entice Fanny to a deep part of the
river. And Fanny can't speak or call for help. Suddenly she disappears.

ALEXANDER   I don't want to live here.

AMANDA   You promised I could start at the ballet school
in the autumn. I'll only stay on condition that I can
move in September.

FANNY   I think we've got a horrid stepfather.

ALEXANDER   That sister of his is off her head.

AMANDA   To say nothing of that mountain of flesh that has to be fed.

FANNY   I'm hungry, Mama.

(EMILIE *sits for a few moments in silence, blinking. Then she puts both hands to her face but checks herself. She smiles at* FANNY)

EMILIE   You must give me time! There is much that has to be changed. Some things will be done quickly, others will take longer. The main thing is that we don't lose heart, that we stick together.

AMANDA   Why did you marry Uncle Edvard?

EMILIE   I married him because I love him. I love you all too, but I have felt so lonely since your father died. That is the way of it. And now let us sleep. When we are not so tired everything will be better.

(*She embraces and kisses her daughters.* ALEXANDER *proudly rebuffs his mother, regarding her coldly.* EMILIE *bends over him all the same, surrounding him with her nice smell and smiling at him*)

EMILIE   Don't act Hamlet, my son. I am not Queen Gertrude, your kind stepfather is no king of Denmark, and this is not Elsinore Castle, even if it does look gloomy.

(ALEXANDER *flings himself back in bed and screws up his eyes; he is furious. His mother stands for a moment looking at him then goes out, closing the door behind her. At first the darkness is dense, but soon the light of the late spring evening breaks through the painted blinds.*

The children whisper to each other, then ALEXANDER *comes padding in and cuddles down in* FANNY'S *bed. After tossing and turning for a while they take their pillows and go over to* AMANDA, *who makes room for them in her bed. They fall asleep almost at once)*

I—Events of the Summer

(The EKDAHL *families spend the summer of 1909 at Eknäset just as they always have done. Everything is the same, yet not the same.* EMILIE *and her children are not there. The house is silent and dead.*

    HELENA, *who is a lady, makes out that she never sleeps. At the moment, however, she is dozing. She is sitting in a comfortable basket chair on the glassed-in veranda, a rug over her knees. One foot is in plaster and is resting on a stool. Her book has fallen to the floor. She holds herself well even when asleep; her mouth is closed and her pale calm face leans against the cushion. Gentle but steady summer rain is falling on the thick greenery that encloses the house and almost blocks the view of the bay. Off and on the thunder mutters halfheartedly over the water. The rain trickles down the panes; there is a gurgling and splashing from the drainpipes and the water butts. The glass veranda is like a diving bell submerged in a green, translucent sea.* HELENA *has been lulled to sleep by the summer rain. The security of childhood, the days pass, suddenly you are old. The rain patters on the roof, the child slumbers. It is also the old woman's sleep. No time has passed. The grandfather clock ticks, clears its throat, and strikes—doing its duty although hours and minutes no longer exist. The house is empty, deserted. Deep in dreamless repose* HELENA *is enveloped by the summer veranda's scents of meadow flowers, aging basket chairs and sun-drenched floorboards. Through a half-open window wafts the smell of heavy, wet greenery, of the water in the bay, of the summer afternoon's transience.*

The telephone on the table beside HELENA's *chair rings. The old lady wakens immediately [she hasn't been asleep at all of course, she has just rested with her eyes closed; besides the book was so wretchedly boring—one of those modern authors with their proletarian tone]. Wide awake at once,* HELENA *has her voice under complete control as she lifts the receiver and answers with a well-modulated hello)*

HELENA　Why, it's you, old Isak! How kind of you to ring. No, you're not disturbing me in the least. I was just sitting with my eyes closed. Everyone has deserted me. It's the annual excursion to Black Rock. Gustav Adolf wouldn't change anything if it was raining cats and dogs. They left at ten o'clock. The weather was still fine then, but clouds banked up over the mainland. They are out with both boats. There's not a soul here. The maids are with them too. What do you think? Tradition is tradition. Won't you come here for once in a way? Oh, do come, and don't be so obstinate. You can't sit there in that awful old shop of yours the whole summer. You'll become as dusty as all the paraphernalia you surround yourself with. You want me to come to you? My dear, I've been sitting here for the last three weeks with my foot in plaster. I was playing hopscotch with Fanny, so I've only myself to blame. I'm not complaining; I have everything I want. I can be by myself, and there's nothing I like better. What did you say? There's a crackling on the line; I can't hear what you say. There's thunder somewhere, but I don't think it's coming this way. Yes,

exactly. Exactly, my friend. Try to do a little spying.
I'm worried. I'm very worried indeed, I may tell you.
No, we haven't heard anything. Emilie merely told us
that she and the children would be staying in town
over the summer. The bishop is not going to take a
holiday. Apparently he's writing a thesis. Oh, that
crackling again! Can't you make one or two discreet
inquiries? Haven't the children been to see you?
There's something wrong, Isak. I feel ill when I think
of that great gloomy house with its thick walls. It's no
place for children to spend the summer. I can't hear
a word you say. Call me up again in an hour or so. Or
I'll call you. That's better. Hello, hello, hello. Oh,
bother it! Can you hear me, Isak? You sound awfully
far away. I'll hang up now and call you in an hour.

(HELENA *puts down the receiver and gives a vexed sigh.*
Thunder rumbles in the distance. The rain is heavier now and
wind stirs the dark greenery. The window blows open and
HELENA *has to get up, lean over the table, and close it. Her*
face and hands get wet)

HELENA   I think I'll make myself a cup of cocoa.

(*She nods confirmingly. An excellent idea. A cup of cocoa and*
one of VEGA's *crisp Danish pastries. She is about to put her*
plan into effect when someone comes through the dining room.
This someone stops tactfully out of sight by the linen cup-
board)

HELENA   Who is it?

MAJ   It's only me, Mrs. Ekdahl.

HELENA   Is it Maj? Come in, my dear. How nice.

(MAJ *steps out on to the veranda. She is in an advanced state*
of pregnancy, but is pretty and well dressed. The thick red
hair has been done up into a demure bun. She has thrown a

light coat over her shoulders. Her freckled face is wet with the rain)

MAJ   Good afternoon, Mrs. Ekdahl. I hope I'm not disturbing you.

HELENA   Not at all, my dear. Give me a kiss. There. Very pretty, very pretty. Did you make it yourself? Such nice material, and a beautiful pattern.

MAJ   Yes, I made it myself.

HELENA   So you didn't go on the excursion?

MAJ *(Laughing)*   There's no room for me in the boat with my big belly.

HELENA   Nonsense, Maj. Is it Alma?

MAJ   No, no, Alma is very kind.

HELENA   Then it's Lydia? Yes, of course.

MAJ   I don't want there to be any fuss. It's all rather tricky.

HELENA   I see. Let's make some cocoa. Vega has baked pastries for the outing.

MAJ   Oh, thank you.

HELENA   What is it, Maj? Is something wrong?

MAJ   Maybe I'm silly to worry.

HELENA   You're worried about the children?

MAJ *(Nods)*   Amanda and I agreed to write to each other. I've already written seven letters.

HELENA   And not had an answer?

MAJ   A postcard. Three weeks ago. Here it is.

(MAJ *hands* HELENA *a postcard with a picture of the main building of the botanical garden. On the back* AMANDA *has written a message: "Dear Maj. We are well. Uncle Edvard took us on an outing today to the botanical garden. We have learned much about rare flowers. Thank you for your letters. I'll write when I get time. Love from Amanda. Fanny and Alexander send their love."*

HELENA *has forgotten the cocoa and the pastries and sunk down in her chair. She sits in thought for a while, holding the postcard. She examines it front and back, as if a secret message were concealed there. Then, with a quick smile, she gives it back to* MAJ)

HELENA   I think we're misjudging Emilie. She is capable of looking after her children herself. We're worrying for no reason.

MAJ   I came to the family before Fanny was born. They're my children too.

HELENA   Are you going already?

MAJ   As I knew you were alone I wanted—I wanted to speak to you, Mrs. Ekdahl.

HELENA   Stay a little longer.

MAJ   Thank you, that's awfully kind of you, Mrs. Ekdahl, but I promised to have dinner ready when they come home and I haven't put the roast in the oven yet.

(HELENA *looks sharply at the young woman, who immediately begins to cry. She lifts her arm to her face and cries as gently and steadily as the summer rain*)

HELENA   Sit down.

MAJ (*Shaking her head*)   No, thank you.

HELENA   Are things so difficult?

MAJ *(Sighs faintly, weeps)* Yes, they are.

HELENA Is it the coffee shop?

MAJ That too.

HELENA Gustav Adolf has been pestering you, I gather.

MAJ *(Nods, weeps)* I don't want to hurt him. He's so kind. *(Pause, cries)* What worries me most is the children. I'm sorry to be crying. I'm behaving badly. Forgive me.

(She bobs to HELENA *and goes out through the dining room)*

II

(It is raining and thundering in town just as at Eknäset. The nursery is dark and chilly and damp; a meager fire is turning to embers in the tiled stove. FANNY *is playing listlessly with the old-fashioned doll's house.* AMANDA *is reading a thick book with Gothic letters and colored plates. It is Grimms' fairytales.* ALEXANDER *is sitting at the table with his head in his hands. He is watching the rain against the square window, the cobblestones in the narrow yard, the well with its iron cupola, and the prison gray wall opposite.*

A key is turned in the door and JUSTINE *comes in with the children's supper on a tray: three bowls of gruel and three slices of coarse dark bread)*

JUSTINE When you've had your supper you are to go straight to bed. The tray can be left until tomorrow. I asked His Grace if you were to be locked in tomorrow too but he didn't answer. Miss Tander sent you some jam tarts. I won't half get into trouble if Miss Vergérus finds out I gave them to you. I'll put them here.

AMANDA   Hasn't Mama come back?

JUSTINE   No, Mrs. Vergérus has not come back.

(JUSTINE *stands by the table with her skinny arms folded over her breast. She smiles pityingly*)

FANNY   I want Mama to come back.

ALEXANDER   Stop harping. She said she'd come this evening if there was a train. Otherwise she'll come tomorrow.

JUSTINE *(Sighing)*   I haven't been very long in this house, thank the Lord, but Miss Tander, who was cook here even in the first wife's day, she could tell you a thing or two.

(*The children have gathered round the table and begun reluctantly to spoon up the skin-covered gruel, after having munched the tough jam tarts.* JUSTINE *wanders about, closing the damper, killing a fly, taking the bedspreads off the girls' beds, hanging up a few articles of clothing. She obviously wants to say something, but hesitates*)

ALEXANDER   Would you like a jam tart?

JUSTINE   Yes, please.

(*She goes over to the table, snatches the tart he holds out, and eats it greedily; her head is bent and her stomach sticks out*)

ALEXANDER   What is it Miss Tander says?

JUSTINE   She says it was the same in the first wife's day. Only worse.

(Nobody says anything. The rain patters against the window and there is a distant mutter of thunder. Although it is only three o'clock in the afternoon the room is half in darkness)

JUSTINE *(After a pause)*   Poor children.

AMANDA   Do you mean us?

JUSTINE   No, I don't mean you. I mean the poor little ones who found their grave in the dark water. Their mother tried to save them but was drawn down by the eddies. They found them later by the bridge. They were clinging tightly to each other, as if they were one body. Their arms had to be sawn off so they could be laid in separate coffins. Since then it has never been really quiet in this house, Miss Tander says.

AMANDA   There are no such things as ghosts.

*(*FANNY *and* ALEXANDER *exchange looks.* JUSTINE *strikes her breast with her lean, long hand and shakes her head)*

JUSTINE   Heaven knows I don't want to frighten anyone, but this house does funny things to you. Look at my left hand: The skin has been eaten away. That's raw flesh. I was taking his morning coffee to His Grace and when I took hold of the door handle the skin stuck to it and was torn off. And *(Whispering)* then someone gave a laugh. I heard it quite plainly, so I turned round, but *there was nobody there.* And I feel sorry for anyone who has to. . . . But I'd better keep quiet and not chatter so much. I'll lock the door now but don't worry, your mother is sure to be back by tomorrow and then His Grace in person will come and set you free. Go straight to bed now and have a good sleep, it'll help the time to pass. The tray can stay till the morning.

ALEXANDER   I've seen them, I have.

FANNY   Seen who?

ALEXANDER   The woman and the children, of course.

AMANDA   Alexander is at his stories again.

ALEXANDER   I *have* seen them. Word of honor.

(JUSTINE, *who is on her way out of the door, shuts it slowly and returns to the table*)

JUSTINE   Is it true?

ALEXANDER   On my word of honor as a Swedish citizen.

AMANDA   There are no such things as ghosts.

FANNY   Don't be silly, Amanda. There are no ghosts but there are *apparitions*. Everybody knows that. It's even in the Bible.

(JUSTINE *sits down on a stool that she fishes out with her right leg. Only her head sticks up over the edge of the table.* ALEXANDER *has his audience*)

ALEXANDER   If you don't want me to tell you I won't, of course. But Fanny knows I'm telling the truth.

(FANNY *nods mysteriously.* AMANDA *looks incredulously at her brother and sister as if it were all a conspiracy to frighten her.* JUSTINE *smiles, but the smile never reaches her eyes*)

FANNY   'Cause I've seen them too.

ALEXANDER   But you weren't there when the woman spoke.

JUSTINE   Oh, so she spoke to you?

ALEXANDER   What I have to tell is of course terrible, and you must all swear not to breathe a word of what I am going to reveal.

FANNY *(Faithful supporter)*   Where did you see them?

ALEXANDER   I had just been in the library with that man
who is married to my mother. He had lectured me for
my bad marks for the German essay and I was passing
through the dining room. The sun was shining. The
room was unusually bright, with a funny sort of light.
Then I saw one of the little girls in the doorway. She
ran past on tiptoe and didn't make a sound. Then came
the other girl, the elder one with the dark hair and the
big eyes. She stopped and looked at me and signed to
me to turn around. And there behind my back, in the
bright sunlight, stood the woman herself in her black
dress. She told me in a faint, faint voice not to be afraid
and said she had something to relate.

(ALEXANDER *pauses for effect, breaks off a piece of the black
bread, and begins to chew it. He seems suddenly to have lost
interest in the whole story and looks absently out of the
window)*

AMANDA   You're lying just to show off.

FANNY   If you don't want to listen you can go into
Alexander's room and shut the door and stop your
ears.

JUSTINE   What did she say?

ALEXANDER   I don't want to frighten anyone but these
were her very words: "I want you to know our secret.
Your stepfather, my husband, locked me and my children into the bedroom. He kept us without food and
water for five days and nights. In our misery we decided to escape. We tied the sheets together and tried
to climb down from the window to the small tongue
of land sticking out into the deep swirling water. My
daughters went first but they fell headlong into the

water and were dragged under. I tried to save them but was sucked into a black whirlpool that caught my clothes. Underwater I was able to grasp my children's hands and draw them to me."

(ALEXANDER *looks at his audience. His sad and horrible drama has been a success.* JUSTINE *gets up, shakes her head several times, and pushes her hand out.* AMANDA *smiles wanly and would like to say something sarcastic but is too deeply affected.* FANNY *stares lovingly and admiringly at her brother)*

FANNY   Well I'm damned.

ALEXANDER   It is a heavy secret we share.

JUSTINE   Go to bed, all of you. Go to bed, and I'll lock the door.

AMANDA   What's the time?

JUSTINE   It's a few minutes past three in the afternoon. I heard the cathedral clock. His Grace has forbidden me to talk to you. I'm not supposed to tell you what the time is. You'll upset me, Alexander, if you can't keep quiet. You and all your stories. *(Angrily)* Go to bed, I said. Go to bed and keep quiet.

(She hurries out and bangs the door. The sound echoes in the stone passage. The key rattles in the lock. The children hear JUSTINE*'s quick footsteps getting fainter and fainter. The rain is still pouring down over the narrow yard with the well, over the bishop's palace, over the town, over the plain, and over the sea that meets the plain with islands, bays, and skerries)*

ALEXANDER   Isak said to me once: "Man may seem little and insignificant but he bears chasms, heavens, and eternities within him. The pity of it is that he cannot perceive his greatness. The pity of it is that his insignificance is always before his eyes. He rarely makes the most of his real capacity." That's what Uncle Isak once said to me when I had the measles.

AMANDA You don't understand what you're talking about.

ALEXANDER I can learn anything by heart. I can make use of my knowledge when I'm older and understand what I've learnt.

AMANDA Maj told me about an idiot who only needed to hear the sermon *once* and could then gabble it off word for word without having the least idea what it was about.

FANNY If you're so afraid of what can't be seen you'd better get yourself another brother and sister.

AMANDA Certain things should not be spoken of.

ALEXANDER "There are more things in heaven and earth, Horatio . . ."

AMANDA *(Shouts)* Oh, do shut up for once!

(ALEXANDER *goes into his partitioned-off triangle and shuts the door. He pulls the quilt over his head and stares through a crack out at the world and reality.* FANNY *opens the door a tiny bit. He beckons to her to come in and makes room for her in the bed. They cuddle up together)*

FANNY Tell me something horrible that has happened to you lately.

ALEXANDER A few nights ago I had a tummyache and had to go to the lav. I went down the passage past the bedroom. The door wasn't shut and the lamps were alight on the bedside tables. His Grace, the bishop,

you know, the one who says he is our stepfather, was
lying on top of mama with his nightshirt drawn up
over his skinny arse, jerking up and down and making
the whole bed shake. Mama was calling for help and
praying to God. "God, oh dear God," she moaned just
like this.

(*There is a knock at the door.* ALEXANDER *breaks off and calls,
"Come in!" It is* AMANDA, *in nightgown and pigtail. She
looks small and miserable standing there*)

ALEXANDER   And what do you want?

AMANDA   I was just wondering if Fanny is coming to
bed.

FANNY   Fanny's already in bed.

AMANDA   The old hag says we're not to sleep in the same
bed.

FANNY   I don't care.

ALEXANDER   There's room for you too.

AMANDA   I'm all shivery; I think I have a temperature.

ALEXANDER   Come on, hop in.

(AMANDA *runs over and gets into bed.* FANNY *lies in the
middle. The quilt covers their fragile security. The windowpanes rattle. The rain pours down*)

ALEXANDER   That was a flash of lightning.

FANNY   It was quite close.

AMANDA   What an awful clap of thunder.

ALEXANDER   I hope the bloody cathedral fell down.

AMANDA   Supposing God punishes you for saying that.

ALEXANDER   If a big know-all like God almighty punishes a skinny runt like Alexander for so little, then he's just the dirty bastard I suspect he is.

FANNY   That's what I think too.

(The faint notes of a flute, the hiss of the rain, and the dying rumble of the thunder, make their way through the thick walls down to the children in their warm cave)

AMANDA   Listen!

FANNY   He's playing the flute.

ALEXANDER   His Grace, the bishop, is playing his flute while he thinks out new ways of tormenting his wife and his stepchildren. If the three of us concentrate on making him die, then die he will. But we must all start together. One, two, three. Die, you bastard! Let's try again. One, two, three. Die, you bastard!

(But the gentle lament of the flute continues to float through the gloom of the big house.
JUSTINE has done her hair and tidied herself: Her collar and cuffs are freshly ironed; she has changed her clogs for her black Sunday shoes, and she has tied a newly starched apron over her black dress. She knocks cautiously on the door of the bishop's study. The notes of the flute cease almost at once. She hears heavy footsteps and the door opens)

EDVARD   Oh, it is you, Justine.

JUSTINE   Please sir, Miss Tander wants to know if Your Grace will be having supper alone after evensong or if there will be a guest.

EDVARD   Tell Miss Tander that I don't want any supper. It will do if you put a glass of milk and a sandwich in the bedroom.

JUSTINE   Thank you, sir. I'll tell her.

EDVARD   Was there something else?

JUSTINE   I don't know.

EDVARD   Hm?

JUSTINE   I don't know if I ought to say anything. It's so unpleasant. And it might seem as if I was telling tales . . .

EDVARD   Well?

JUSTINE   Please sir, I can't stand here in the door if . . .

EDVARD *(Curtly)*   Come in then. And shut the door.

(BISHOP VERSÉRUS's *study is full of tobacco smoke and melancholy, discomfort and anguish. The heavy furnishings clash openly or regard each other with sullen contempt. In the middle of the floor, on the shabby threadbare carpet, is a music stand with the flute and the sheet music of a suite by Telemann. In front of the stand is a chair with a low back and tall legs. A lighted paraffin lamp blinks sleepily, intensifying rather than lessening the gray, rainy murkiness. The cathedral clock is just striking four. Far below the dirty green windows of the study the river surges past, brownish black and swirling, with white-crested wavelets. The bishop sits on the chair in front of the music stand)*

EDVARD   Well, what is it that is so important?

JUSTINE   Please sir, you said I was to keep an eye on the children and listen to their talk and report if I heard anything special.

EDVARD   Well?

JUSTINE   Alexander made up a terrible story.

EDVARD   Oh?

JUSTINE   It was about. . . . Oh, it's awful. I don't know how to get it out.

(BISHOP VERGÉRUS *picks up his flute and blows a few notes. He turns the pages and appears uninterested*)

JUSTINE *(Whispering)*   He says, sir, that you locked your first wife up and that she was drowned with her children when she tried to escape through the window.

(BISHOP VERGÉRUS's *face swells to a remarkable size. The hand holding the flute trembles. He lays it down carefully on the music stand, gets up, takes a few steps, and stops in front of the open fireplace, where no fire has burnt for many years*)

EDVARD   Well?

JUSTINE   That's all, sir.

EDVARD   You can go.

JUSTINE   Thank you, sir.

(*She bobs and leaves the room, closing the door.* BISHOP VERGÉRUS *goes over and stands by the window. His face is still swollen*)

III

(HELENA *is seized by an unaccountable melancholy, which is so strong that she contemplates the idea of having a little cry. She sits upright in the chair and tries out a few deep sighs. The tears fill her eyes.*

The rain surrounds her body and her mind. It trickles down

*the windowpanes but also over her thoughts and the mental
pictures moving behind her eyes. The ripple of rain in the big
trees and on the roof has a safe, soothing sound, but it is the
safety of an old habit from childhood, and therefore tinged
with sadness.* It shows I'm getting old, *Helena thinks,
satisfied in some way with the thought, as after all she can
see through her predicament and is thus mistress of the situation. She wipes her tears away with the back of her hand and
when she has blinked a few times she can see much more
clearly. Sitting opposite her is her son,* OSCAR EKDAHL, *in his
crumpled linen suit. He has put his shabby old summer cap
on the table and is looking at her fondly.*)

HELENA   Yes, Oscar, that's just how it is. One is old and
a child at the same time, and cannot understand what
became of all those long years in between that were
considered so important. Here I sit growing melancholy and thinking that the time was all too short.
Your father used to say I was sentimental. As you
know, he was not particularly sensitive and was both
angry and indignant when he died. He never thought
life was cruel or unfair or beautiful. He just lived and
made no comments. He left those to me. And when I
thought that life was this, that, and the other he
laughed at me and said I was sentimental. But heavens
above, I was an actress. And as an actress I *had* to be
emotional. Oscar, my dear, I may be distressing myself for no reason. When you have nothing to occupy
your thoughts you immediately start worrying. May
I take your hand?

(OSCAR *gives her his hand and she holds it for a long time in
hers. With the other hand she encloses his wrist, feeling the
even beat of the pulse)*

HELENA   I remember your hand when you were a child.
It was small and firm and dry, and your wrist was so

awfully slender. I enjoyed being a mother. I enjoyed being an actress too, but I preferred being a mother. I liked being pregnant and didn't care tuppence for the theater then. For that matter everything is acting. Some parts are nice, others not so nice. I played a mother. I played Juliet, Ophelia. Suddenly I am playing the part of a widow. Or a grandmother. One part follows the other. The thing is not to scamp. Not to shirk. But what became of it all, can you tell me that, my boy?

(HELENA does not really expect an answer. She never has, and all her life this has been generally understood)

HELENA   You're a good boy to listen to your old mother's soliloquies, as Isak calls them. Yes, you're a good boy, Oscar, and I grieved terribly when you died. That was a strange part to play. My feelings came from my body and although I could control them they shattered reality, if you know what I mean. *(Pause)* Reality has been broken ever since, and oddly enough it feels better that way. So I don't bother to mend it. I just don't care if nothing makes sense.

(OSCAR is still holding her hand. He has turned his face to the window. His smile has faded; he is serious now and looks tired and worn out, as HELENA remembers him from his last years)

HELENA   Oscar, my boy?

OSCAR   Yes, Mama?

HELENA   You look depressed and ill.

OSCAR   I'm worried.

HELENA   Are you worried about Emilie and the children?

(The veranda door is pushed open. Perhaps HELENA wakens at the sound, perhaps she has not been asleep. OSCAR has gone.

It is growing light over the bay; the rain has lessened and the thunder has died away. In the doorway stands a small person in yellow oilskins. Her long fair hair is damp and plaited in two thick pigtails. She is barefoot. She regards HELENA *with pleased surprise)*

EVA   Are you alone?

HELENA   Yes, I am alone.

EVA   My name's Eva and I live over there on the other side.

HELENA   How old are you?

EVA   Eight.

HELENA   Would you like some lemonade?

EVA   No, thank you.

HELENA   Or some cake?

EVA   No, thank you.

HELENA   What is it you want?

EVA   I want to know when Fanny and Alexander are coming this summer. We usually play together and it's dull when they're not here.

HELENA   I don't know. *(Pause)* I just don't know.

EVA   Oh.

HELENA   I don't know.

   (EVA *stands for a few moments pondering over this incredible and disappointing news)*

EVA   Can't you *tell* them to come?

HELENA   Perhaps I ought to.

EVA   Nobody would dare to say no to you.

HELENA   Oh?

EVA   That's what Papa says anyway.

HELENA   Won't you come in and sit down?

EVA   No, thank you. I must go now. Good-bye.

HELENA   Good-bye then, Eva.

EVA   Don't forget you've promised.

HELENA   I'll do what I can.

(EVA *stands a moment gazing at* HELENA. *Then she says good-bye once more and jumps down the veranda steps, one at a time. Suddenly the little patch of yellow is swallowed up by all the greenery. The rain ripples, a dog barks in the distance.* HELENA *reaches for her book and begins listlessly to cut pages with a heavy silver paper knife. Someone moves in the hall on the other side of the dining room, a door opens, footsteps are heard.)*

HELENA   Who's there?

EMILIE   It's only me.

HELENA   Emilie!

(They embrace affectionately. HELENA *pats* EMILIE'*s hair and strokes her cheek)*

EMILIE   I had such a longing to come.

HELENA   Are the children with you?

EMILIE   No.

HELENA   Are they well?

EMILIE   *(After a pause)*   I don't think so.

IV

(At the same time, with the same rain falling, BISHOP ED-
VARD VERGÉRUS *opens the trial of his stepson* ALEXANDER
EKDAHL. *The prosecutor's chief witness is* JUSTINE, *the housemaid. The proceedings are conducted in the presence of the
bishop's mother,* BLENDA VERGÉRUS, *his sister* HENRIETTA,
the sisters of the accused AMANDA *and* FANNY, *and God
Almighty in Heaven.*

*It all begins with the children's being fetched. The door is
unlocked and* HENRIETTA *and* BLENDA *enter the nursery.
They wake the children by shaking them roughly and order
them to get dressed immediately.* FANNY *begins to cry,*
AMANDA *asks where their mother is, and* ALEXANDER *demands to know what is going on. No one answers their
questions. Tight lips and grim faces. When* AMANDA *has put
on a dress they march off to the library, where* BISHOP VER-
GÉRUS *is waiting together with* JUSTINE.

BLENDA *and* HENRIETTA *seat themselves on the sofa, each
with her handwork. The children have stopped by the door.*
BISHOP VERGÉRUS *gets up from the long library table;* JUS-
TINE *gives a brief, uncertain smile.* ALEXANDER *is told to step
forward. He stands in the middle of the vast room, which is
filled with books from floor to ceiling. A great dread, like a
sick crab, squirms in his bowels)*

EDVARD *(Gently)*   Alexander, my boy. In the presence of
your sisters and Justine you have accused me of having
murdered my wife and my children.

ALEXANDER   It's not true.

EDVARD   Justine, please repeat what you told me.

JUSTINE   Alexander said he had seen the late Mrs. Vergérus and her children. She had spoken to him. She
had said that in a fit of wrath His Grace the bishop had

locked her and the children into the bedroom without food or water. On the fifth day they tried to escape through the window but were drowned.

EDVARD Do you recognize the story, Alexander?

ALEXANDER No, sir.

EDVARD So you allege that Justine has given a false testimony?

ALEXANDER She was probably dreaming.

EDVARD Justine, are you prepared to confirm your statement on oath?

JUSTINE *(Bobbing)* Yes, Your Grace.

EDVARD That is good, Justine. Did Fanny and Amanda hear Alexander's story?

AMANDA No.

FANNY *(Whispers)* Stop pinching. *(Aloud, to* BISHOP VERGÉRUS) No.

EDVARD So you deny having heard anything?

AMANDA I only remember that Justine told us that the mother and children were found under the cathedral bridge and that they had to be sawn apart to get them into the coffins.

EDVARD Did you say that, Justine?

JUSTINE *(Whispers)* Yes, sir.

(There is a long silence. BISHOP VERGÉRUS*'s face swells until it is huge, terrible, and inhuman. His voice is nevertheless unchanged—quiet and friendly)*

EDVARD *(To* ALEXANDER) You maintain that Justine was lying or dreaming?

ALEXANDER   Yes, sir.

EDVARD   Are you prepared to take an oath on it?

ALEXANDER   Of course.

EDVARD   It is a mortal sin to swear falsely, Alexander. It is called perjury and is severely punished.

ALEXANDER   Oh, is it?

(ALEXANDER *shifts his weight on to the other leg, puts his hand at his side, and licks his dry lips. Nothing matters now. Life is over. God's punishment is going to strike him. Bloody damn vindictive God*)

EDVARD   Kindly come here to the table. Lay your left hand on the Bible and say after me: "I, Alexander Ekdahl, swear by Holy Writ and by the living God..."

ALEXANDER (*In a firm voice*)   "I, Alexander Ekdahl, swear by Holy Writ and by the living God . . ."

EDVARD   ". . . that everything I have said, am saying, and will say is the Truth and nothing but the Truth."

ALEXANDER   ". . . that everything I have said, am saying, and will say is the Truth and nothing but the Truth." May I go now?

EDVARD   Do you want to go already, Alexander?

ALEXANDER   There's nothing more to say. How can Justine prove she wasn't dreaming?

EDVARD   Tell me something. Are you happy here with us in the bishop's palace?

ALEXANDER   As happy as a snake in an anthill. Though worse.

EDVARD   You dislike your stepfather, don't you?

ALEXANDER   Must I answer?

EDVARD   Do you remember that the two of us had rather an important little talk about a year ago. It concerned certain moral questions.

ALEXANDER   You can't call it a talk.

EDVARD   What do you mean?

ALEXANDER   The bishop did the talking and Alexander said nothing.

EDVARD   Said nothing and felt ashamed, perhaps. Of his lies.

ALEXANDER   I've grown wiser since then.

EDVARD   You mean you lie better.

ALEXANDER   That's one way of putting it.

EDVARD   I don't know what you imagine, Alexander. Do you think this is a joke? Do you think you can smirch another person's honor with impunity? Do you think you can lie and play the hypocrite and commit perjury and get away with it? Do you think we are having a game, Alexander? Or do you think perhaps that this is a kind of play in which we say whatever lines come into our heads?

ALEXANDER   I think the bishop hates Alexander. That's what I think.

EDVARD   Oh, so that is what you think. *(Pause)* Well, I'll tell you something, my boy. Something that will perhaps surprise you. I don't hate you. I love you. But the love I feel for you and your mother and your sisters is not blind and is not sloppy. It is strong and harsh, Alexander. If I must punish you, I suffer more than you know. But my love for you compels me to be truthful. It compels me to chasten and form you even if it hurts me. Do you hear what I say, Alexander?

ALEXANDER No.

EDVARD You are hardening your heart. Moreover you are misjudging the situation. I am much stronger than you are.

ALEXANDER I don't doubt that!

EDVARD Spiritually stronger, my boy. It's because I have truth and justice on my side. I know that you will confess in a little while. Your confession and your punishment will be a relief to you, and when your mother returns this evening it will all be over and done with and life will go on as usual. You are a wise little man, Alexander. You realize that the game is up, but you are proud and stubborn, and of course you are ashamed.

ALEXANDER One of us should be ashamed. That is true.

EDVARD You must understand that your insolence does not help your cause. It merely confirms my suspicions.

ALEXANDER I've forgotten what it is I am to confess.

EDVARD Oh. *Have* you now.

ALEXANDER *(After a long pause)* What does the bishop want Alexander to confess?

EDVARD You know that I have means at my disposal.

ALEXANDER I didn't know, but I do now.

EDVARD Effective means.

ALEXANDER That doesn't sound pleasant.

EDVARD In my childhood parents were not so soft-hearted. Naughty boys were punished in an exemplary but loving manner. With the cane. The motto was: "Spare the rod and spoil the child." I have a cane too. It is there on the table. Then we had another means that was really efficacious, and that was castor oil. There you see the bottle, Alexander, and a glass. When you've swallowed a few mouthfuls of that you will be a little more docile. And if castor oil didn't help there was a dark and chilly bogey hole where one had to sit for a few hours, until the mice started sniffing at one's face. You see, over there under the stairs, Alexander, a nice big hole is waiting for you. Then of course there were other, more barbarous methods, but I disapprove of them. They were humiliating and dangerous and are not applied—nowadays.

ALEXANDER   What punishment will I get if I confess?

EDVARD   You may decide that for yourself, Alexander.

ALEXANDER   Why must I be punished?

EDVARD   That is perfectly obvious, my boy. You have a weakness in your character—you cannot distinguish lies from truth. As yet you are a child and your lies are a child's lies, however dreadful they may be. But soon you will be a grown-up man and life punishes liars ruthlessly and indiscriminately. The punishment is to teach you a love of truth.

ALEXANDER   I confess I made that up about the bishop locking his wife and children in.

EDVARD   Do you also confess that you have committed perjury?

ALEXANDER   Yes, I suppose so.

EDVARD   Now you have won a great victory, my boy. A victory over yourself. Which punishment do you choose?

ALEXANDER   How many strokes of the cane do I get?

EDVARD   Not less than ten.

ALEXANDER   Then I choose the cane.

EDVARD   Take your pants down. Bend over by the sofa. Put one of the cushions under your stomach.

(Ten not too hard strokes of the cane follow. ALEXANDER *makes no sound. He bites his hand, tears fill his eyes, his nose runs, he is dark red in the face, and blood oozes from the weals in his skin)*

EDVARD   Stand up, Alexander. *(*ALEXANDER *stands up)* You have something to say to me.

ALEXANDER   No.

EDVARD   You must ask my forgiveness.

ALEXANDER   Never.

EDVARD   Then I must whip you until you think better of it. Can you not spare us both such an unpleasant experience?

ALEXANDER   I'll never ask your forgiveness.

EDVARD   You won't ask my forgiveness?

ALEXANDER   No.

EDVARD   Take your pants down. Bend over the sofa. Put a cushion under your stomach. *(Raises his arm to strike)*

ALEXANDER   No more, please!

EDVARD   Then you beg my forgiveness?

ALEXANDER   Yes.

EDVARD   Button your pants. Blow your nose. Lend him a handkerchief, Justine. What have you to say, Alexander?

ALEXANDER   Alexander begs the bishop's forgiveness.

EDVARD   For the lies and the perjury.

ALEXANDER   For the lies and the perjury.

EDVARD   You understand that I have punished you out of love.

ALEXANDER   Yes.

EDVARD   Kiss my hand, Alexander!

ALEXANDER *(Kissing* BISHOP VERGÉRUS*'s hand)*   May I go to bed now?

EDVARD   Yes, my boy, you may. But so that you will have an opportunity of thinking over the day's events in peace and quiet, you are to sleep in the attic. Justine will provide a mattress and a blanket. At six o'clock tomorrow morning Henrietta will unlock the door and you are free. Is that understood, Alexander?

ALEXANDER   Yes, Your Grace.

V

(EMILIE *and* HELENA *are sitting opposite each other, holding one another's hands and talking quietly, almost in a whisper.*

It is still raining over the bay, over the plain, over the summer veranda. The afternoon light is soft and shadowless, all outlines are distinct, all contrasts mellow. The clock in the dining room strikes)

HELENA   Must you go already?

EMILIE   I have been away too long.

HELENA   Poor Emilie.

EMILIE *(Shaking her head)*   It's worst for the children. They are punished for the slightest misdemeanor. Henrietta locks them in and forces them to go to bed in the middle of the day. A week ago Fanny refused to eat up her porridge. She was made to sit there all evening. She was sick at the table. At last she ate it.

HELENA   Alexander?

EMILIE   He is mad with jealousy but doesn't realize it is mutual.

HELENA   My poor Emilie!

EMILIE   I am tormented by a boundless self-contempt. How could I be so blind? How could I feel sorry for that man? After all I'm an actress and should have seen through his dissimulation. But he was cleverer than I was. His conviction was greater than mine and he dazzled me. I had been living alone so long, ever since Fanny's birth. I hated my occasional emotional storms. I hated the terrible loneliness of my body. Oscar was my best friend, you know that, Helena. You know how fond of him I was; you know that my grief was sincere when he left us. But you also know that we never touched each other.

HELENA   I reproach you for nothing.

EMILIE I thought that my life was finished, sealed up. Sometimes I grieved, but blamed myself for my ingratitude. What is the time, Helena? I must go soon; I'm so afraid of being late. His rage is terrible. I don't know how a man can live with so much hate. I saw nothing; I was too dense. He spoke to me of another life—a life of demands, of purity, of joy in the performance of duty. I had never heard such words. There seemed to be a light around him when he talked to me. At the same time I saw that he was lonely, that he was unhappy, haunted by fear and bad dreams. He assured me that I would save him. He said that together with the children we would live a life in God's nearness—in the truth. *That* was the most important, I think—what he said about the truth. I was so thirsty —it sounds dramatic and overstrung, Helena, I know, but I can't find any other word—I thirsted for the truth. I felt I had been living a lie. I also knew that the children needed a father, who could support them and guide them with a firm hand. *(Pause)* He would also free me from my physical loneliness. I was so grateful, Helena. And I left my old life without regret. Now I must go. A carriage is waiting up by the gate. I am afraid that something may have happened while I have been here. I go in constant dread that Alexander may say something that displeases him. Alexander is so foolhardy. I have tried to warn him, but he can't see that his stepfather is a dangerous opponent who is merely waiting for the right opportunity to crush him.

HELENA You must leave him, Emilie.

EMILIE *(Smiling)* I knew you'd say that. Every hour I think I ought to leave him, sue for a divorce, go back to the theater and our family.

HELENA If you are so sure it ought not to be impossible.

EMILIE I am pregnant, Helena!

HELENA Nevertheless you should . . .

EMILIE Forgive me for interrupting you. I shall briefly relate all the facts. I have asked him for a divorce. He refuses. He says not only that he loves me but that a divorce is unthinkable in his position. I tell him I'll leave him just the same. Then he gets out the statute book and explains in detail what will happen: In a court of law I will lose, on grounds of "desertion," as it is called. The children will be taken from me, to be brought up by him. I have written in secret to a lawyer who is my friend. He has confirmed what Edvard says. I am shut in and can no longer breathe. I am dying, Helena. And I hate that man so violently that I could —*(Silence)*

HELENA *(Whispering)* We must find a solution.

EMILIE Don't tell anyone I've been here. Not a soul!

VI

*(*ALEXANDER *has slept for an hour or two. When he wakes up it is still light; he can see the colorless summer sky through the skylight. He tries to sit up but it hurts and he prefers to lie on his side with his hands between his thighs.*

He is exhausted with emotion, has a splitting headache and a raging thirst.

The attic loses itself in darkness and shadows. The air is thick with dust and heat; there is a smell of old wood, rotten apples, and dead mice. The pale light falls over the chimney and the mattress and ALEXANDER. *This is a place for specters and ghosts.* ALEXANDER *knows it)*

ALEXANDER *(Faintly)* Mama.

(The old rafters snap, a floorboard creaks. Is that a dim figure standing over there?)

ALEXANDER *(Faintly)* Mama.

(A soft flapping of wings. Then a gust of wind. A deep sigh passes through the big room. ALEXANDER *seems to hear whispering voices, or is it only the wind?)*

ALEXANDER *(Clearing his throat)* Papa. Can you hear me? If you are coming to see me please remember I'm afraid of ghosts and that you are in fact dead. Don't come from behind, please, and don't suddenly put your hand on my shoulder. I might go out of my mind with fear, and you don't want me to do that, do you? *(Pause, silence)* I want you to come from in front and to have your usual voice and your usual clothes, and please don't have any special glaring light, I couldn't bear that either. *(Pause. He listens)* I don't understand why I have to see dead people when it makes me ill. A schoolmate of mine would give almost anything to see a ghost but has never seen one in his life, in spite of spending all night in a cemetery.

(ALEXANDER *stops speaking and listens. Unmistakable footsteps over there in the dark. "Bloody hell," he says with a shudder. "Bloody hell. Oh Jesus, I'm dying of horror." He*

holds his breath and shuts his eyes tightly. When he opens them a girl of about ten is standing in front of him. She gazes at him with burning eyes. Her face is narrow and she has two thin plaits at her ears. The colors of her dress are faded; she is wearing thick woolen stockings with a hole in one knee and high winter boots. She is holding her hands behind her back. At least that is how it appears. It can also be that she has no arms)

PAULINE   My name is Pauline. My sister Esmeralda is over there by the green screen. She is angry with you, Alexander. She wants us to punish you. Why do you look so surprised? You know quite well why we are angry with you.

ALEXANDER   I've no idea why.

PAULINE   You have lied about your father. You have said that he locked us in. It is not true. The sluice gates at Mill Bridge had been closed for several weeks and the river was frozen over. We had been given new skates for Christmas. But the ice broke and we fell in. Mama tried to save us but the current dragged us under the ice. Now you know the truth, you wretched boy. I and my sister have been trying to think of a good way of scaring you as a punishment for your lies, and we have found something that will frighten you more than anything else.

ALEXANDER   Please don't frighten me.

PAULINE   Do you hear what he says, Esmeralda?

(ESMERALDA *invisible, titters*)

PAULINE   We were fond of our father. He was always kind to us. We can see how you are tormenting him with your hate.

ALEXANDER   I don't hate him.

PAULINE   Do you hear what he says, Esmeralda? He doesn't hate our father! (ESMERALDA *titters again, still invisible*) We've thought out a way of rescuing our father from you and your nasty hatred. We're going to frighten you until you go mad and are shut up in the asylum and put in a padded cell with chains round your hands and feet. We shall come and see you. *(Whispers something in* ALEXANDER*'s ear. He gives a shrill scream)* That's only the beginning!

*(*ESMERALDA *giggles. She can now be faintly seen. Suddenly angry voices can be heard and footsteps that are real and not at all ghostly. A key is put in the lock of the attic door and* EMILIE *rushes up the steps. She has not even stopped to take off her coat and hat. When she catches sight of* ALEXANDER *huddling by the chimney, she gives a dull roar and throws her arms round him. She touches the bloodstained shirt and the weals on his buttocks, but she does not cry. Nor does* ALEXANDER. *He is aware of his mother's powerlessness and senses the danger that will engulf them like a dark wave. He knows too that there are people who want to harm him and do away with him, and that those are the people who have the power to carry out their evil intent. Reality has always supplied building stones for* ALEXANDER*'s dreams and fantasies. Suddenly reality comes crashing down into his consciousness with blind brutality. Enclosed in this howling fear he nevertheless feels the will to survive. He glimpses the days and the years full of dread and lies, but also of resistance and modest victories.*

Mother and son totter down the steep steps of the attic. FANNY *and* AMANDA *are waiting by the door. For a moment they hold each other tightly as if they were one body.* ALEXANDER *can see* PAULINE *standing by the chimney. Her face is distorted with hatred)*

VII

(HELENA *has found it chilly on the veranda and has moved into the dining room. She is sitting at the big table with an album and several envelopes containing photographs. The old lady examines each one meticulously, making a note on the back in her neat flowing hand of what it is and if possible when it was taken. If the person is dead she makes a little cross and adds the year. When she has registered and dated the picture in this way she puts it into a thick leather-bound album with frames and clasps and gold-tooling on the covers. This occupation is soothing and disposes* HELENA *to a gentle melancholy. Her husband, the elder Oscar Ekdahl, was an eager amateur photographer. He took thousands of pictures with several cameras, both snapshots and posed studio portraits. He liked to develop and print his glass negatives but he was not particularly interested in sorting the photos and sticking them into albums. In time* HELENA *undertook this task, occasionally with mixed feelings since Oscar's photographic zeal also included unknown beauties of doubtful reputation.*

The newly bought phonograph on its pedestal is producing Caruso's melting tones. It is still raining but now and then the sun peeps out, transforming the landscape. There is a rainbow over the bay and the grandfather clock strikes five.

Happy voices, laughter, and shouts can now be heard from the jetty. Soon doors are opened and shut in the other houses and there are quick footsteps on the gravel. JENNY *is having a heated argument with her mother.* MAJ *says something to* PETRA; VEGA *and* ESTER *approach chattering and puffing. They open the back door and move about noisily in the kitchen;* HELENA *can hear what they are saying.* VEGA *has been stung by a wasp and her leg has swollen.* ESTER *makes a compress and says that a wasp sting is worse than snakebite and that* VEGA *must keep still and that she,* ESTER, *will see to the mistress's supper. Then the veranda door opens and* GUSTAV ADOLF *and* ALMA *come in, red-cheeked with the sea air and plenty of drink. They kiss* HELENA *and ask how she is and whether she has been lonely. She replies that she is very well and has quite enjoyed being on her own.* GUSTAV ADOLF *and* ALMA *are in high spirits and rattle on)*

ALMA Vega was bitten by a wasp.

GUSTAV ADOLF A wasp stings, my sweet. It has a sting just like your old man.

ALMA And Petra fell in and was soaked to the skin. She slipped on the rocks, silly girl, and slid right down into the water.

GUSTAV ADOLF Lucky her behind is so well padded. She takes after you, Alma my poppet.

ALMA *(Laughing)* He's been going on like that all day. I don't know what's got into him. *(Yelps)* Ow! You're *not* to pinch my bottom!

GUSTAV ADOLF And Mama is busy with old Oscar's photographs. How many thousand have you sorted by this time?

HELENA Anyway here is a picture of you and your brothers. You can't have been more than five there.

GUSTAV ADOLF You can see already which of the brothers is . . .

ALMA *(Pointing to a photograph)* Who is that beautiful woman?

HELENA Has it been raining on you all the time?

GUSTAV ADOLF Not a drop, Mama dear. Out in the archipelago there wasn't a cloud in the sky. But we saw the rain over the mainland and heard the thunder.

HELENA   Here it has been raining all day.

GUSTAV ADOLF   That woman with the décolletage I remember very well. She was one of Papa's lady friends.

ALMA   If you like, I will look in for a while after supper. I'll bring my handwork.

GUSTAV ADOLF   She smelt so confoundedly nice that little woman.

HELENA   You're mistaken. We were at school together. She married a Count Ekenstierna and had twelve children and grew the size of a house. She died last winter.

GUSTAV ADOLF   Mama, I have always admired the adroit way you handled Papa's amours. *(Kisses her)*

ALMA   We must go now.

GUSTAV ADOLF   I'm going into town tomorrow morning. Can I do anything for you?

HELENA   Thank you, Gusten dear, I don't need anything, but I'd like to talk to you about Maj.

GUSTAV ADOLF   Christ, what now. She's got all she wants, hasn't she?

HELENA   Are you sure, Gusten?

GUSTAV ADOLF   Hell and damnation. I'm sorry, Mama, but what more does that girl . . .

ALMA   Quiet, Gusten. The moment Maj is mentioned he loses his temper and begins to shout and carry on.

HELENA   You must realize, Gusten dear, that Maj is not your private plaything. Thanks to Alma's broadmindedness she has become a member of our family and she is expecting my grandchild. In your dictatorial way you have mapped out her future. It may be that . . .

GUSTAV ADOLF *(Angrily)*   I'm bloody well sure that Alma and . . .

ALMA   I don't like your swearing in your mother's presence, do you hear, Gusten?

GUSTAV ADOLF *(Angrily)*   I like the girl. I wish her well. I want to ensure her future. I don't want her to be dependent on the family's goodwill if I should pop off. She has agreed to my suggestions. Damn it all, she doesn't need any protectors, especially not *against me!* Don't try to make out I'm dictatorial. Maj has decided everything herself. I like her. I'm kind to her. Alma is kind to her. I'm bloody hurt, let me tell you. Bloody hurt. There's not the slightest reason to side with Maj against me. I'm fond of her. Alma is fond of her. She is loved in the same way as Fanny and Petra are. Oh yes, I can see your looks. Not *quite* like the other children. But almost. She's good to me; she doesn't think I'm fat and old and disgusting. No one does, for that matter. Gustav Adolf Ekdahl has a soft spot for the ladies. What's to be done about that? Maj is to go her own way through life and I shall give her firm ground to stand on. Now, that's enough said about that. Come along, Alma, let's go home and have supper. The opera singer said something about looking in with his wife and children. Good-bye, Mama. Give me a kiss. I don't want you and Alma to sit tattling about Maj's future. I'll see to that. Or rather, she will. Good night, Mama. Don't be cross with me for shouting. It's only those skinny old crows out in the kitchen who hear and it will cheer them up having something to chatter about. Come along, Alma.

ALMA *(Kiss)* I'll come back in an hour or two.

GUSTAV ADOLF Like hell you will.

HELENA I'll be glad to see you, even if it's late.

ALMA Calm down now, Gusten, or you'll have a stroke.
You're purple in the face.

(They go off bickering. GUSTAV ADOLF *repeats his arguments
and* ALMA *reproaches him for swearing, for his dictatorial
nature and his loud voice.* VEGA *appears in the doorway and
asks if she may serve supper.* HELENA *thanks her and says she
is not hungry, but that* VEGA *can put some stout and a veal
sandwich beside her bed. Then they talk about* VEGA's *wasp
in particular and the danger of wasps generally. When the
subject is exhausted,* VEGA *withdraws. She goes and sits on the
sunset bench under the big oak tree together with* ESTER. *The
rain has ceased and a warm evening breeze stirs the darkening
greenery.*

PETRA *can be heard playing the piano. The windows are
open to the mosquitoes and the sunset and the sound quivers
in the evening light.* HELENA *has returned to the veranda. She
has lost interest in Oscar's photographs but neither books,
patience, nor handwork tempts her. Sadness and anxiety rise
and fall with her breathing.* [Something terrible is about
to happen, and here I sit, powerless.]

She hears footsteps and voices. It is CARL *and* LYDIA,
come to pay their evening call. HELENA *sighs with boredom.
I can't cope with those people. She can see them on the
garden path. They have walked quickly up the slope and*
CARL *has to stop and get his breath.* LYDIA *stands beside him
with her hands behind her back and her head sticking forward)*

LYDIA *I'm* not going to say anything.

CARL If you don't say anything, who is to?

LYDIA   Not I, anyway.

CARL   Nor I.

LYDIA   You can't expect me to say anything.

CARL   Mama distrusts me, you know that. She distrusts me and it's your fault. So I can't say . . .

LYDIA   If she distrusts me, *mein Carlchen*, then I don't see how I can say anything at all.

CARL   You must tell her I'm in despair.

LYDIA   You can say that better yourself, *mein Carlchen*.

CARL   You're a prize idiot, Lydia. You must make it clear to her that I'm thinking of committing suicide.

LYDIA *(Weeping)*   Is that really true? We can live together poor. I will work . . .

CARL   Idiot. Nitwit. Imbecile. I *shall* work.

LYDIA   What do you want me to say, *mein Carlchen?*

CARL   Have you no imagination? Numskull. Say you have seen that I'm unhappy. That I've stopped eating. That I lie awake at night.

LYDIA   Yes, you do lie awake with insomnia.

CARL   It damn well is insomnia. Say I've grown so quiet. That I never laugh. That when I do laugh it sounds horrible, do you get that? A talk between women. Don't say it in so many words, but you can hint that I have spoken of suicide.

LYDIA   You're not to say that awful word or I'll start to cry, *mein Carlchen*.

CARL   Fathead.

LYDIA   *Do* you think of suicide, *mein Schatz?*

CARL   Only when I see you.

LYDIA   Why are you so cruel?

CARL   Don't go, for Christ's sake. *(Snarling)* Where are you going?

LYDIA   I *won't* talk to your mother. I'm going home. *Du bist böse, böse.* I must cry. You don't understand that I love you. Now I'm crying and I won't be able to stop.

CARL   Dear God in Heaven! Why must I go on acting in this wretched farce. Lydia! Don't run! Wait!

(LYDIA *stretches her arms above her head, sobs loudly, and trips over her skirt.* CARL *tugs at her to make her stop but fails and falls headlong.* LYDIA *utters a little shriek and is immediately at his side, helping him to his feet and dusting him down. Soon they disappear behind the lilac arbor.*

HELENA *turns round.* JENNY *is standing in the room, bare-legged, bare-armed, suntanned, and chubby. She is wearing a faded floral nightgown and is gazing at her grandmother attentively. She is holding something behind her back)*

HELENA   You should have been in bed long ago.

JENNY   I crept out.

HELENA   What do you think your mother will say to that?

JENNY   She won't know about it. Unless you tell tales of course.

HELENA   What do you want with your old granny?

(JENNY *takes a step forward, then another. She lays a straw threaded with wild strawberries in front of* HELENA, *smiles and runs off)*

VIII

(EMILIE *is lying on* AMANDA*'s bed. She has not taken off her coat.* ALEXANDER *is cuddled up at her side with his head on her arm.* FANNY *is sitting at the foot of the bed and* AMANDA *has taken up a strategic position by the door to the passage. Long silence. Dusk is falling.* BISHOP VERGÉRUS*'s steps are now heard. He opens the door without knocking and stops on the threshold)*

EDVARD   Welcome home, Emilie. You've been away a long time. *(Pause)* We were beginning to worry. *(Pause)* Miss Tander is wondering if you would like something to eat.

EMILIE   I'm not hungry.

EDVARD   I'll tell her then. *(Pause)* Are you coming to bed soon? *(Pause)* It is late.

EMILIE   I'll come when the children are asleep.

EDVARD   I'll sit in the library and read in the meantime. Please don't be too long. *(Pause)* Good night, children. Actually we had agreed that Alexander was to sleep in the attic tonight, but I gather the decision has been changed.

EMILIE   Yes. *(Pause)* It has been changed.

EDVARD   I see. Oh well, perhaps it is better like this. Good night, Fanny.

FANNY   Good night, Uncle Edvard.

EDVARD   Good night, Amanda.

AMANDA   Good night, Uncle Edvard.

EDVARD   Good night, Alexander. (ALEXANDER *doesn't answer*) Is he asleep?

ALEXANDER   No, I'm not asleep.

EDVARD   Then you can answer me when I wish you good night.

ALEXANDER   No, I can't.

EDVARD   Can't? *(Smiles)* What nonsense is that, Alexander?

ALEXANDER   Alexander does not wish the bishop a good night.

EDVARD *(Laughing)*   You have a sense of humor, Alexander, and I like that.

(BISHOP VERGÉRUS *laughs still more and shuts the door. His footsteps grow fainter. Mother and children lie in silence, all in their own thoughts. A single lamp is alight by the bishop's armchair. The vast room rests in darkness. It is night.* EDVARD VERGÉRUS *is reading a church magazine. He makes notes in the margin with a pencil. He is wearing gold-rimmed glasses and a smoking jacket. A wisp of smoke rises from his pipe. He has stretched out his legs over a stool that belongs to the armchair.*

EMILIE *is sitting at the big table, which is cluttered with books and newspapers. She still has her coat on. Her hat has disappeared somewhere along the way)*

EDVARD   Did you see your mother-in-law and your relations? Was it a pleasant visit? Did it rain? Here it has been raining and thundering all day. Oh well, we could do with it. At least the farmers could. Alexander and I had a little passage of arms this afternoon. It was the same old thing. He finds it hard to differentiate between fantasy and reality. But we sorted it all out.

At least in part. Alexander is not stupid. He is not stupid, but he doesn't forgive easily. *(Laughs)* "Alexander does not wish the bishop a good night." That is really priceless. In one way I appreciate his character. He is quite the little eccentric. You say nothing, Emilie. *(Pause)* Are you cross about something? You have absolutely no reason to be. In fact I am the one to reproach you.

EMILIE   You're crazy.

EDVARD *(Smiling)*   I must confess I find you least attractive when you make an effort to be vulgar. As I said, there are one or two things I could ask about, but I don't want to pick a quarrel, so I'll hold my peace.

EMILIE   You lock the children in.

EDVARD   A safety measure, Emilie. I wanted a guarantee that you would come back.

EMILIE   You ill-treated Alexander.

EDVARD   You express yourself so dramatically, dear Emilie. I punished him. That is part of my duty in bringing him up. Moreover, the punishment was mild in relation to the crime.

EMILIE   He is bleeding and the skin has been stripped off . . .

EDVARD   Forgive my interrupting you. I gave him a few strokes. His buttocks will be sore for a few days but it is a healthy soreness. The young man will think twice about fabricating any new lies—or *fantasies*, if you prefer to call them that.

EMILIE   And the humiliation?

EDVARD   God humbles us in punishment. It may seem humiliating but it is necessary. Besides, Emilie, a loving punishment can never be humiliating in the deeper sense. Love and consideration have nothing in common and the language of love can be fairly harsh.

EMILIE   *You* speak of love.

EDVARD   You permit yourself to be sarcastic. *(Pause)* Shall we terminate this conversation and go to bed?

EMILIE   You locked him into the attic.

EDVARD   Of course. He needed to be alone.

EMILIE   You know he's afraid of the dark.

EDVARD   The nights are light at this time of the year and those with a clear conscience have nothing to fear.

EMILIE   I could kill you.

EDVARD   You will harm the child with such thoughts.

EMILIE   Our child will never be born.

EDVARD   Be careful what you say, Emilie. *(Pause)* A mother who in morbid hatred of her husband wants to destroy her child, what is to be done with a mother like that? *(Pause)* The asylum, Emilie.

EMILIE   You don't frighten me.

EDVARD   I must frighten you. But I do it with a heavy heart, since I love you in spite of everything. *(Gets up and goes over to her)* Get it into your head once and for all that you must obey me, that you must submit, that you must be alive to your obligations as wife and mother. You are not strong, Emilie, and pregnancy is weakening you. From now on you are to stay in a room that we shall prepare for you as comfortably as possible. Henrietta and my mother will take it in turns to look after you. For the time being your liberty will be somewhat restricted. We must be very careful. *(Pause)* You must also know that the slightest attempt on your part to rebel or get in touch with the outside world will affect your children's well-being. You are pale with hatred and rage, Emilie. I advise you to be calm and courageous. You have been living in an artificial world, entangled in artificial feelings. I must teach you and your children to live in reality. It is not my fault that reality is a hell. In this world, Emilie, in this reality Jesus Christ was tortured and put to death. *(Pause)* Through your irresponsibility you have compelled *me* to take the responsibility, not only for your children but also for you. It is heavy and I feel a terrible loneliness.

(EMILIE *stifles a scream*)

EDVARD *(With tenderness)*   I am an ordinary man with big failings but I discharge a mighty office. The office is always greater than the one who performs it. The man who lives in an official position is its slave. He has no right to opinions of his own. He is there for his fellow men and only in his submission is he alive. His slavery is his freedom. I love you, Emilie. I love you more than anyone else in this world, as God is my witness. But you are threatening my office by your insane and dangerous attempts to break away and by your constant talk of divorce. All that must be suppressed, Emilie. You must learn humbly to bow yourself under the power we both serve.

(EMILIE *screams*. EDVARD *strikes her across the mouth*)

EMILIE   I curse you. I curse your child that I am carrying. I shall tear it out with my own hands and crush it as one crushes a poisonous animal. Every day, every hour I shall wish you dead and I shall think out a torment that is more horrible than anything the human mind can conceive.

EDVARD   We are passing through the Vale of Tears, Emilie. We are passing through the Vale of Tears and making it rich in springs.

I—The Demons

(On a hot September day a cart lumbers into the bishop's yard. ISAK JACOBI, *in hat and winter overcoat, is sitting beside the driver. Two young men are lying in the bottom of the cart, puffing in the heat and drinking beer. The Jew tells the driver to wait and goes and bangs on the door. It is opened by* HENRIETTA. *She stares at the visitor with distaste)*

HENRIETTA   Good afternoon, Mr. Jacobi.

ISAK   Good afternoon, Miss Vergérus. I hope I am not . . .

HENRIETTA   What do you want?

ISAK   I was wondering whether His Grace is . . .

HENRIETTA   He is writing his sermon and must not be disturbed.

ISAK   Then perhaps it is possible to speak to his wife?

HENRIETTA   She is indisposed and is resting in her room.

ISAK   And must not be disturbed?

HENRIETTA   My mother is out and I myself have no time.

ISAK   I am not so sure that . . .

HENRIETTA   I am sorry, Mr. Jacobi.

ISAK   It is possible that His Grace would be annoyed if I were not permitted to state my . . .

HENRIETTA   What is it about?

ISAK   Some months ago, in November to be exact, His Grace was kind enough to propose a business deal to me.

HENRIETTA   Really? I cannot recall it.

ISAK   Of course not, Miss Vergérus. His Grace is sure to spare his family such trivial worries.

HENRIETTA   What worries is my brother likely to have that could concern you, Mr. Jacobi?

ISAK   Oh dear, Miss Vergérus. Please don't force me to be vulgar.

HENRIETTA   You are an unpleasant man, Mr. Jacobi. Moreover, you have an insinuating and insulting tone. I have neither time nor inclination to enter into a conversation with you. And that is all I have to say. Farewell, Mr. Jacobi.

ISAK   A pecuniary embarrassment.

HENRIETTA   I beg your pardon?

ISAK   Your brother, His Grace the bishop, found himself in a pecuniary embarrassment. May I come in?

(HENRIETTA *opens the door a little wider*)

ISAK *(Stepping inside)*   Thank you. How kind of you. Allow me to compliment you on your dress, Miss Vergérus. That is no cheap material. From Paris, no doubt.

HENRIETTA   What business have you with my brother, Mr. Jacobi?

ISAK   May I sit down?

HENRIETTA   Sit there. No, not there. There.

ISAK   In some strange way, I don't know why, I appreciate your straightforwardness.

HENRIETTA   And I do *not* appreciate your fawning, Mr. Jacobi. Now then, what business have you with my brother?

ISAK   None at all, so far as I know.

HENRIETTA   I'm tired of your riddles. Tell me what is on your mind and go.

ISAK   I must first speak to His Grace.

HENRIETTA   He has forbidden me to disturb him.

ISAK   If you would be kind enough to show me the way, I will do the disturbing. *(Smiles, whispers)* It's a matter of money, Miss Vergérus. A great deal of money.

HENRIETTA   Does my brother owe you money?

ISAK *(Appalled)*   On the contrary, my dear lady! On the contrary! This is the way of it, Miss Vergérus. In November, His Grace wanted to borrow money. Regrettably, the Jew has certain principles—for example, never to lend money to the clergy. It can be risky, as it were, in the long run. His Grace then suggested a transaction. That I should buy a fine chest and a very handsome cupboard for a reasonable sum. I declined.

HENRIETTA   Oh, I see. So you declined the transaction.

ISAK   Yes, foolishly, as I have changed my mind. I should like nothing so well as to buy those two pieces. For almost any price at all. *(Whispers)* Almost.

HENRIETTA *(After a long pause)*   I shall get my brother.

(She goes away. ISAK JACOBI *is out of the chair in a flash. In squeaking galoshes he slinks from room to room and emerges into the long stone passage. He tries one door after the other, finds one that is locked, digs in the pocket of his overcoat and gets out a bunch of oddly shaped keys.* BISHOP VERGÉRUS'S *voice can now be heard in a distant part of the house. "I told you not to disturb me."* HENRIETTA *mumbles something and the bishop replies, "Yes, of course, he clings like a leech."* ISAK *tries one of the keys in the lock and the door swings open almost immediately. Inside stand* AMANDA, FANNY, *and* ALEXANDER, *looking in alarm at* ISAK, *who is now in a great hurry)*

ISAK   Stay where you are. I'll come and get you in a few minutes. Take your shoes off.

(He closes the door and rushes back through the rooms to the chair in the hall. BISHOP VERGÉRUS *regards him darkly.* HENRIETTA *can be glimpsed behind her brother)*

ISAK   Forgive me. An old man's unfortunate weakness. Forgive me. Good afternoon, Your Grace.

EDVARD   You wish to buy the chest and the cupboard?

ISAK   That is so, Your Grace.

EDVARD   And what will you give me for them?

ISAK *(Drawing out an agreement)*   Here is the sum.

EDVARD *(Reading)*   You have indeed changed your mind.

ISAK   I may have an interested buyer.

EDVARD   It is too little.

ISAK   In that case I am sorry. *(Prepares to go)* Farewell, Your Grace. Farewell, Miss Vergérus.

EDVARD   You're up to some mischief. Your kind are always up to some mischief.

ISAK   Farewell. I apologize most humbly.

EDVARD   The two pieces are worth at least double.

ISAK   Without a doubt, Your Grace. Regrettably, however, a poor antique dealer in the provinces cannot offer the correct sum.

EDVARD   I am being cheated.

ISAK   Your Grace is free to refuse and is thus not being cheated. I thank you for sparing me the time and beg to withdraw. I hope I have not disturbed you unduly.

EDVARD   Have you the money with you?

ISAK   The money? Oh yes, the money—the purchase sum. Of course, Your Grace. The sum mentioned on the paper is in my breast pocket. Here are the big notes.

EDVARD   Give me the money, Mr. Jacobi.

ISAK   Of course. At once. If I may have Your Grace's esteemed name on the contract? *(Hands over the money)*

EDVARD   I will see to it, Mr. Jacobi. I will see to it.

(BISHOP VERGÉRUS *goes away, reading the paper. The door is closed)*

ISAK Miss Vergérus, will you graciously permit me to set to work? May I ask my men to come up and remove the pieces?

HENRIETTA *(Shrugging)* As far as I am concerned.

(ISAK *hurries to the window and calls to the men, who promptly obey.* HENRIETTA *stands for a few moments with her index finger pressed to her lips, regarding the bowing* ISAK)

HENRIETTA You will forgive me if I withdraw?

ISAK I shall miss you, my dear lady.

HENRIETTA I presume you will not take anything that is not your due.

ISAK *(Smiling)* Suspicions recoil on those who harbor them.

(HENRIETTA *is on the point of retorting but checks herself and sweeps out of the room. She goes through the dining room and the drawing room and suddenly vanishes.* ISAK JACOBI *darts out into the stone passage, flings open the door of the children's room, and signals to them to make haste. They get up from the floor with their shoes in their hands, staring uncertainly)*

ISAK *(Whispering)* Hurry. There's no time to lose.

(*He takes* AMANDA *by the hand and pulls her along. The others follow. They are now standing in the banquet hall.* ISAK *opens a huge wooden chest and whispers to the children to climb in. At that moment the door opens and* BISHOP VER-GÉRGUS *comes in.* ISAK *shuts the chest, the children are in safe keeping)*

ISAK I presume Your Grace wants to make sure that I am not taking away anything that is not my due. *(Opens the lid of the chest)* Please have a look.

EDVARD   Oh, that is quite all right. I just wanted to give
you back the signed contract.

(ISAK *closes the lid of the chest and sits down. The men have
begun to maneuver the cupboard out, having taken the doors
off the hinges and removed the top.* BISHOP VERGÉRUS *wraps
his dressing gown round his legs and sits down beside* ISAK.
He smiles amiably. ISAK JACOBI *returns the smile*)

EDVARD   What do you say about that picture over there?

ISAK   An authentic van Meertens, apparently.

EDVARD   Would it interest you?

ISAK   An extremely beautiful work. Unfortunately I am
not an art dealer.

EDVARD   A good price?

ISAK   My resources are rather strained at the moment.
How is your wife?

EDVARD   How kind of you to inquire. My wife is indisposed. The sudden heat does not agree with her.

ISAK   Would it be possible to pay my respects in
person?

EDVARD   No, I am sorry.

ISAK   I understand. Here is a letter to her from old Mrs.
Ekdahl.

EDVARD   I shall give it to her.

ISAK   That is more than kind of you.

EDVARD   You damned Jewish swine. (*Grabs* ISAK *by the
collar*) You damned filthy, loathsome Jewish swine.
You thought you could trick me. You abominable
hook-nosed skunk.

(With great strength BISHOP VERGÉRUS *lifts* ISAK JACOBI *up from the chest and hurls him to the floor. Then he gets up and throws open the lid of the chest. It is empty. He stares into it, then rushes after the men to stop them. The cupboard gapes doorless and empty.* ISAK *is sitting on the floor fiddling with his glasses, which have been broken in the fall. A door opens to an adjoining room and Mrs. Blenda Vergérus appears. Farther in, brightly illumined by the setting sun, the shapeless* ELSA BERGIUS *is sprawled among her pillows)*

ELSA *(Screams)* What's going on? What's going on? What's going on?

BLENDA What's going on?

EDVARD *(Furious)* That swine is trying to steal my children.

HENRIETTA It's not possible. I have the key of the nursery.

*(*BISHOP VERGÉRUS *tears open the door to the nursery.* AMANDA, FANNY, *and* ALEXANDER *are lying huddled on the floor, as though asleep. Their faces are pale in the sunset light. The bishop bends over them—perhaps they are dead. He raises his hand to touch* ALEXANDER*'s brow)*

EMILIE Don't touch them!

*(*EMILIE *standing over by the stairs, heavy with her advanced pregnancy, sweaty and unkempt in a stained dressing gown. Her dishevelled hair hangs loosely round her sunken face; her lips are sore and bloodstained but her eyes are calm and cold —an aging Ophelia who unhappily refrained from gathering flowers by the stream)*

EMILIE If you touch them, I will kill you.

*(*ISAK JACOBI *has got to his feet. He brushes down his black coat and makes soothing gestures. The men carry out the*

cupboard. BISHOP VERGÉRUS *clenches his hands and goes into his study, closing the door.* BLENDA *feeds the grunting* ELSA BERGIUS. HENRIETTA *lifts the lid of the chest. It is still empty. She sinks into a chair and regards* EMILIE *spitefully. The old Jew smiles absently but looks somewhat tired. He staggers over to* EMILIE, *supporting himself against the wall and trying out his broken glasses. The men begin to carry out the chest. It is heavy)*

II

(The men go off after having carried the chest into a dark, untidy room behind the shop. ISAK JACOBI *pulls down the torn blinds, locks the front door, and opens the lid. The children climb out, dirty and shaken but safe and sound. The Jew lays a finger on his lips and signals to them to follow him up a spiral staircase that twists through two floors full of every imaginable object under the sun.*

The staircase ends in a narrow hall opening onto a dark and shabby dining room cluttered with old-fashioned furniture. The table is laid and the candelabra are alight. A young man of about twenty, with pale face and gentle eyes, greets them in silence)

ISAK   Aron, my nephew.

*(*ARON *bows politely and hurries out into the kitchen, where he fetches a large tureen with steaming broth. They all sit down at the table.* ISAK JACOBI *distributes the bread and ladles the soup. No one breaks the silence. A summer fly*

buzzes against the dirty window. Somewhere, far away, a man's voice is humming a monotonous song with unusual intervals)

ALEXANDER   Can the bishop fetch us back?

ISAK *(Shaking his head)*   In a day or two he will negotiate with your uncles. For the moment there is no danger.

FANNY   I want Mama.

ISAK *(Stroking her hair)*   Patience, Miss Ekdahl. Patience.

AMANDA   How long are we to stay?

ISAK   Hardly all your lives.

ALEXANDER   I'm sleepy.

ISAK   Our guests are tired, Aron! Have you aired and tidied the room and made the beds? Have you put flowers?

ARON   I have carried out all your orders, Uncle.

(They get up from the table and go through a long dark passage that seems to extend toward the back of the house)

ISAK   Has Ismael eaten?

ARON   I gave him his dinner at three o'clock.

ISAK   Behind this door lives my other nephew, Ismael. He is ill, so he must be locked up. This door must always be kept shut. Remember, Alexander. Remember, Fanny and Amanda.

(The children nod, silent and dejected. ISAK *pats* AMANDA's *cheek and looks grave)*

ISAK   Sometimes he sings. At night too. It is nothing to worry about. You will get used to it.

(ISAK *motions to them and they go on through the long passage, which opens into a large room with no other furniture but a dozen chairs standing in two rows on a worn Persian carpet. At the end of the room is a puppet theater. Everywhere, on the stage and along the walls, hang puppets in motley costumes. They regard the newcomers with dark, fixed eyes in mysteriously pallid faces. The thin daylight making its way in through the half-drawn curtains lends their bodies and limbs, their features and gestures, something powerful and commanding that will not be gainsaid*)

ISAK   Aron's puppet theater. If you ask him nicely he will no doubt give a performance one evening.

(*They pass through a red drawing room with red wallpaper, red carpet, red sofas and armchairs, heavy red curtains. From the ornate ceiling hangs a large chandelier swatched in tulle. Beyond the drawing room is a Chinese cabinet with rice paper on the walls, black-lacquered furniture, and small statuettes. Everything is shabby, dusty, and faded, as though dying.* ARON   *opens a black-painted jib-door to a small room with wide floorboards, a tall window looking out on an autumnal tree, two narrow beds with puffy white quilts, light-colored patterned wallpaper, lace curtains, and a multitude of very small pictures on the walls. In one corner is a washstand behind a battered screen. Three white chairs and a rickety table complete the furniture. A tall paraffin lamp keeps guard over the table and there are rag rugs on the floor. The floor has been newly scrubbed. The window is open and on a small chest of drawers there is a bowl of apples that give out a nice smell*)

ISAK   This will be your home for the time being. I hope you will like it. Lock the door from inside at night and don't open it to anyone. Go to bed now. Aron will help you to close the window. If you want anything, call down this tube. Whistle first, then speak in a clear voice. It's no good shouting because no one will understand what you say. Good night, Amanda. Good night, Fanny. Good night, Alexander. Don't forget to say your prayers.

ALEXANDER   Don't go!

ISAK   You want me to stay for a while?

ALEXANDER   Yes, please.

ISAK   Then I'll sit down on this chair.

ARON   I'll go and see to Ismael. Good night.

CHILDREN   Good night—

ARON   Aron. My name is Aron. My brother's name is Ismael. Our parents died when we were children.

(He smiles politely and goes out without a sound. The children have sat down on one of the beds. They perch there like three ruffled, travel-weary little birds with no shelter for the night. ISAK *looks steadily at them for a long time)*

ISAK   Well? Is it Fanny and Amanda who join forces and have secrets because Alexander is a boy? Or is it Alexander and Fanny who play the same games and think that Amanda has no thought for anything but her dancing? Or can it be that Alexander and Amanda think that Fanny is still a child? How is it now?

ALEXANDER   We stick together. All three.

ISAK   That's as it should be.

FANNY   Amanda wants to be a ballerina.

AMANDA   Our stepfather has forbidden me to learn dancing.

ALEXANDER   He can't forbid you because Grandmamma
has decided you're to be a dancer.

FANNY   When Grandmamma decides anything, that settles it.

ALEXANDER   We get a bit tired of her dancing sometimes,
but we're sorry she's going away. Since Papa died—

ISAK *(After a pause)*   Yes, what?

ALEXANDER   Oh, nothing.

AMANDA   You can't trust grown-ups.

FANNY   They're not all there.

AMANDA   Mama must be out of her mind.

*(The children fall silent. They are tired, uncertain, and de-
spondent.* ISAK *does not want to break the silence. He lights
his pipe and takes a small but thick book out of his torn
pocket. The pages are very thin and closely printed in strange
type)*

ALEXANDER *(Politely)*   What book is that?

ISAK *(Looking up)*   It's a book of stories, thoughts, words
of wisdom, and prayers. It is written in Hebrew.

FANNY   Do you understand that language, Uncle Isak?

ISAK *(Nods)*   Would you like me to read you something?

ALEXANDER   Uncle Isak!

ISAK   Yes?

ALEXANDER   Are you quite sure His Grace can't come
and get us?

ISAK   You can set your mind at rest, Alexander.

FANNY   Go on, read!

ISAK   It will probably be rather halting, as I have to
translate *(Turns the pages, clears his throat, begins to
read):* "You are journeying along an endless highway together with many other people. Wagons drawn by big horses
rattle past, forcing the wanderers and the herds of cattle to
the sides of the road or down into the deep ditches. The road
leads across a stony plain where nothing grows. The fiery
sun burns from morning to evening and nowhere can you
find any coolness or shade. A scorching wind is blowing;
together with all the people, the carts, and the cattle, it stirs
up huge clouds of dust, which chokes your mouth and blinds
your eyes. You are driven forward by a strange anxiety and
you are tormented by a raging thirst. Sometimes you ask
yourself or one of your fellow travelers about the goal for
your pilgrimage but the answer is uncertain and hesitant.
(Pause) Suddenly you are standing in a wood. Night is
falling and all is quiet; perhaps you hear the sleepy cheeping
of a bird, perhaps you hear the sighing of the sunset wind in
the tall trees. You stand in astonishment, full of your anxiety and your distrust. You are alone. You are alone and you
hear nothing because your ears are stopped up by the dust of
the road. You see nothing because your eyes are inflamed by
the merciless glare of the sunlight. Your mouth and throat
are parched by the long journey and your cracked lips are
tightly pressed around curses and harsh words. (Pause) So
you do not hear the ripple of flowing water; you do not see
the flashing stream in the dusk. Blinded, you stand beside it
and do not know it is there. Like a sleepwalker you make
your way along between the pools. Your unseeing skill is
remarkable and soon you are back on the noisy highway in
the burning shadowless light among the bellowing cattle, the
furiously driven wagons, and the embittered people. With a
look of surprise you say to yourself: Here on the highway I
feel safe. In the wood I was all by myself; in the wood it
was lonely and horrible. (Pause) But the evening reflects its
clear eye in the dusk of the wood. The water ripples tire-

lessly as it flows through the woods, becoming brooks, rivers, and deep lakes.

'Where does all this water come from?' the youth asked. 'It comes from a high mountain,' replied the old man. 'It comes from a mountain whose peak is covered by a mighty cloud.' 'What kind of cloud?' the youth asked. The old man replied: 'Every man bears within him hopes, fears, longings. Every man cries his despair aloud. Some pray to a particular god, others utter their shouts into the void. This despair, this hope, this dream of deliverance, all these cries accumulate during thousands and thousands of years; all these tears, all these sacrifices, all these longings collect and condense into a vast cloud round a high mountain. Out of the cloud rain streams down over the mountain, forming the brooks, the streams and the rivers, forming the deep springs where you can slake your thirst, where you can bathe your face, where you can cool your blistered feet. Everyone has at some time heard of the springs and the mountain and the cloud, but most people remain on the dusty highway for fear of not reaching some unknown destination before evening.' "

III

(A few days later diplomatic negotiations are opened between BISHOP VERGÉRUS *and* EMILIE's *former brothers-in-law. The venue is the library of the bishop's palace.* EDVARD VERGÉRUS *is wearing cassock and gold cross. The brothers have put on morning dress. The refreshments consist of dry sherry and biscuits. The autumn sunlight bores through the dusty air, striking the men's faces and turning them waxen)*

EDVARD   Shall we sit down? I recommend the armchair, my dear Carl, and Gustav Adolf will find the sofa the most comfortable. May I tempt you with another drop of sherry? No? An almond biscuit, my sister's speciality? Not that either. I shall sit here in my old easy chair. It has accompanied me ever since my early days as curate in the Amsberg Chapelry in southern Dalarna.

(BISHOP VERGÉRUS *has no more to say. The visitors are silent. The specks of dust whirl in the sunbeams. A fat black cat paces slowly across the carpet, its tail erect and crooked like a walking stick. The men watch the cat*)

EDVARD   I want the children to come back. The town is small. Tongues will soon be wagging.

(*There is again silence. The brothers exchange looks. When* CARL EKDAHL *begins to speak he is very composed.* GUSTAV ADOLF *intersperses his words with brief nods. The black cat has jumped up on the library table and stretched out in a patch of sunlight. He gazes at the meeting with wide-open yellow eyes and ears cocked forward. His tail moves slowly and a stovepipe purr is heard from his belly*)

CARL   I fear that you have misunderstood the reason for our visit. We are here on behalf of the family and ourselves to prevail upon you to release Emilie and the children. We cannot say with certainty that we know what has occurred. All we know is that our dear Emilie is most unhappy and that the children dislike it here.

GUSTAV ADOLF   The family is quite aware that a divorce is a painful step for a highly placed servant of the church, and we will gladly compensate you for the severe loss in a suitable manner. I have had a preliminary talk with my mother and we are prepared to put

a considerable sum at your disposal—money that, of
course, you can use for charity, a foundation, or some
other purpose dear to your heart. We agree with you
that everything must be handled with the greatest
discretion, and my mother has declared herself willing
to undertake a journey to Italy with Emilie and to stay
away for at least a year.

EDVARD   Let me say first that I fully appreciate the respect and generosity that the Ekdahl family is prepared to show me in my affliction. At the same time
it is extremely painful to me, but necessary, to speak
my mind. The children have deserted their home.
They must unconditionally and without waste of time
be restored to their legal parents. Every delay will
cause us all, not least their mother, unspeakable suffering. When the children have been brought back I shall
be prepared to listen to any proposals that the Ekdahl
family may have. Nonetheless, in order to avoid further delay and misunderstanding, I should like to
stress that a divorce is quite out of the question.

CARL   I am very grateful for your precise and unambigu-
ous attitude. At the same time I am compelled to tell
you that the children will never be brought back to the
bishop's palace to be subjected there to the hardships
they have already undergone. I might add that on that
point the Ekdahl family is unanimous. The matter is
thus not open to discussion. The three children were
born within our family and we consider ourselves
responsible for their well-being and development.

EDVARD   It pains me that the Ekdahl family wishes to
dictate, especially bearing in mind that I, as the children's stepfather, have the law on my side. Moreover,
as a dignitary of the church, I have the moral advantage.

GUSTAV ADOLF *(Laughing)* But we have the children, my dear sir.

EDVARD I am glad you are able to laugh in this painful situation. Legal proceedings may be unavoidable after all.

GUSTAV ADOLF I doubt it, dear Edvard! You would rather shit on yourself than face the ignominy when the old crones of your parish begin to whistle between their false teeth. It is possible that you have morality and the law on your side. But you must bear in mind that I am in league with immorality, and even if you happen to emerge the victor in a lawsuit we who stand for immorality shall already have spread so many incredible rumors about your person and your conduct and your household and your sister and your servants and your sanity and your sexual excesses and your false hair and your hypocrisy and your hypochondria and your utter lack of decency that you will be compelled for the rest of your life to apply for a post among heathens and Eskimos. I am not saying this to frighten you, my good sir. I am saying it merely so that we shall have all our cards on the table. So you had better listen to reason, if you're capable of it.

EDVARD Your buffoonery is amusing and I would be inclined to laugh if your blather did not contain what I would call an actual threat.

GUSTAV ADOLF Let me tell you something, my fine friend, something you may not be quite clear about: I can see through you. You are a contemptible blackguard.

CARL Shut up, Gusten, and think of your blood pressure. *(To the bishop)* I must indeed apologize, my dear

Edvard. Even if we have conflicting views concerning what at present seems an insoluble problem, we must behave like sensible people. I dissociate myself entirely from my brother's expressions and attitudes and beg you to be assured that he does *not* represent anyone but himself, and certainly does not speak for the rest of the family.

(BISHOP VERGÉRUS *bows to* CARL *in silence, then leans back in his armchair, drumming on the elbow rest with the long bony fingers of his slender hand. He fixes his blue eyes on a point behind* GUSTAV ADOLF's *left ear. There is a faint smile at the corners of his mouth*)

EDVARD   Well, well. *(Pause)* Well, well.

GUSTAV ADOLF *(With an effort)*   You must please forgive me. I apologize on all fours. I am a boor, or so my wife says. I have no eye for people's inner qualities. I drink too much. I am covered in shame. My apologies.

EDVARD   We'll say no more about it. I am even prepared to respect an honest man's honest opinion, although it may be a trifle . . . uncouth. *(Smiles)* May I pour you a glass of sherry? I assure you it is good.

GUSTAV ADOLF *(Cowed)*   Oh, thank you. Thank you very much. *(Drinks)* I am most awfully sorry. I am so fond of that silly Emilie, that silly actress. We love her, the whole family loves her. Then our brother Oscar died. We didn't take care of her sufficiently. We have a lot to blame ourselves for. One is so damned slack and self-centered. I said so to Alma only this morning: If we had not been so damned slack and self-centered this would never have . . .

(He breaks off and bites his moustache, after a warning signal from CARL. BISHOP VERGÉRUS's thoughts seem to be elsewhere. It is growing dark under the high ceiling, the sun's blaze is *dying, the book-lined walls recede in the gloom. The black cat purrs)*

CARL   In present circumstances I don't see that we can reach an agreement. Let us regard our confidential and candid talk as a preliminary exploration.

EDVARD   I fear that I do not share your cautious optimism. I consider our negotiations broken off and feel compelled to make my standpoint quite clear. The children must be restored to their home within twelve hours. Otherwise—although it goes against my nature and my principles—I shall be forced to report the matter to the police and the public prosecutor.

CARL   If the children *were* brought back, is it conceivable that we might have an informal talk about future arrangements for them and their mother to see their cousins and relations?

EDVARD   I am a believer in fixed rules and principles, a fact that in no way conflicts with my sincere and passionate love of freedom. It is a cornerstone in my Christian faith.

CARL   May I take your utterance as an indirect promise of a further talk on the delicate subject of Emilie and the children's freedom of movement?

EDVARD   *(With a tired smile)*   Disintegration in our life consists very largely of broken ties between people who have the capacity to esteem and love one another. A cruel and puzzling mystery.

GUSTAV ADOLF *(Angry)*   To think that a man of my bulk, with a fully grown beard and in my right mind, has to sit on this ridiculous and uncomfortable chair listening to this unmitigated hypocrite. "Disintegration in our life!" Kiss me where my back changes name. Now you shut up, Carl. You shut up while I tell this puerile mental masturbator what we have up our sleeves. I'm going to tell you something, Edvard Vergérus. *I have bought up your promissory notes!* You didn't know that, did you? Oh yes, my friend. One hundred and ten thousand riksdaler in debts. So I'm the one who dictates the conditions. That took the wind out of your sails. Look how pale he is, the holy man! Look at him, Carl! *(Laughs)* I'm damned if his nose isn't longer too. You're a special kind of rogue, Edvard Vergérus, but one thing I've learnt in my profession and that is to recognize the smell of a rogue, even if he is wearing a cassock. And I know how rogues should be treated. Roughly! Our little Emilie is to have her divorce in a trice or I shall declare His Holiness bankrupt with a vengeance.

*(*GUSTAV ADOLF *must now pause for breath. He is so furious that his cheeks have turned purple. At the same time he is in high spirits and laughs loudly. He stops abruptly, painfully aware that it has grown very silent.* CARL *is huddled in a corner of the sofa regarding his neglected nails.* BISHOP VERGÉRUS*'s smile has broadened somewhat but his deep blue eyes are gazing far away into the dusk. The cat has risen and is drawing its claws along a book cover with a faint rasping sound)*

CARL   Idiot!

GUSTAV ADOLF   Eh?

CARL   I said idiot. *You* are an idiot.

GUSTAV ADOLF   I thought it only fair to tell him he hasn't a chance.

CARL   I get so tired of you sometimes, Gustav Adolf.

GUSTAV ADOLF   Oh. Hm. What have I done now?

CARL   You'll soon see.

(BISHOP VERGÉRUS *returns slowly to consciousness and his visitors. He regards them suddenly with a certain goodwill, almost cordially*)

EDVARD We spoke a moment ago of the advantage of putting our cards on the table. I beg to return to that metaphor presently. To Mr. Ekdahl I'd like to say that I feel sorry for him. He has a very poor and one-sided opinion of the world and the people in it. He is plagued by the all-too-widespread misconception that man is ruled by his needs. He thinks that everything can be bought and sold. Mr. Ekdahl is the son of one of the greatest actresses in the land. Despite this he has grasped little or nothing of the mind's unlimited power over matter. He is a wretched Caliban, groping for his blunt tools with clumsy hands. I am sorry for him; I feel a sincere pity. *(To Carl)* My dear sir, I thank you for a respectful and in every way dignified conversation. I regret that we have not come to an agreement. I valued my contacts with the Ekdahl family and delighted in the warmth and goodwill that flowed toward me. All that is now over. *(Pause)* Try some time to tell your brother—no, he would never understand that there *are* people who have no needs, who are indifferent to money, who disdain the good things of this world, who with joy allow themselves to be slandered and besmirched because their consciences are clear before God the Almighty. *(Short pause)* And now we come to our game of cards, which Mr. Ekdahl spoke of so wittily. Allow me to play the trump card. Excuse me a moment.

(BISHOP VERGÉRUS *bows to the brothers, who have stood up. He hurries across the big stretch of carpet and is swallowed in the gloom. The cat, which has jumped down from its vantage point, rubs against* CARL's *legs, purring loudly*)

GUSTAV ADOLF   That man is made up of the devil himself. Have you ever seen such a cold-blooded knave.

CARL   If you hadn't behaved like . . .

GUSTAV ADOLF   . . . an idiot. I admit it. I'm sorry. That's the wrong word. I'm bloody upset.

CARL   Quiet now. He's coming. Keep your mouth shut.

GUSTAV ADOLF   I swear.

(A curtain is drawn aside and BISHOP VERGÉRUS *enters. He is leading* EMILIE *by the hand. She is wearing a soft dress that hangs in folds and sets off her beauty. Her hair is well combed and plaited. She goes toward her brothers with a happy smile, embraces and kisses them. Her eyes fill with tears)*

EMILIE   Dear, dear Gustav Adolf and dear Carl. How kind of you to come and help us in our quandary. Edvard has told me everything and given me an account of your talk. I can't say how grateful I am for your care and affection. Thank you, thank you. But I'm afraid you've misunderstood it all. Isak Jacobi took it upon himself to abduct the children. It is terrible and unbelievable. It is so nice and safe here. Edvard is so good to us and we are very happy. I implore you with my whole heart to bring the children back.

(Tears well up in EMILIE'*s eyes. She stops for a moment, dabs her lips with a tiny lace handkerchief, and turns away. The brothers stand with hanging arms and blank faces.* BISHOP VERGÉRUS *regards his wife with tenderness. The cat has sat down with its tail curled around its paws. He seems to take no interest in the situation)*

EMILIE   It is true that I have been anxious and unhappy. It is true that I went out to Eknäset and talked to Aunt Helena. It is true that the children have found it hard to adjust themselves to their new surroundings. It is true that in this house we live a stricter and more serious life than at home. But I am happy and secure. Edvard is goodness itself. You must believe me. I implore you! Bring back my children! I cannot live without them. Dear, dear friends. Do as I say. It is all a terrible mistake.

IV

(That same night ALEXANDER *has three strange experiences, which later he never tells anyone about. He wakes up about four in the morning [hears the clock in the cathedral tower, not so close and familiar as at home, not so frightening and deafening as in the bishop's palace, but far off and unreal as in a dream]. He is at once aware that he badly wants to pee. Being overcome by tiredness in the evening he fell asleep in defiance of his good habit and now the need is urgent.* ALEXANDER *has a peculiarity. He talks to himself, especially in critical situations. This is a critical situation)*

ALEXANDER   I want to pee. I must find a potty.

(He gets out of bed clad in ARON's *nightshirt, which is too long for him. He hunts desperately about the room, but there is no chamber pot)*

ALEXANDER   There isn't a potty; I must go to the privy.

(In pressing need, he goes out into the strange apartment. Through the windows a shadowless dawn light is seeping)

ALEXANDER   I hope there aren't any ghosts.

(Everything is confusing: passages and sudden rooms, with junk, furniture, statues, pictures, household utensils, old clothes, curios, and books. He hears muffled snoring. A door is ajar and in a high bed lies Uncle Isak like a king lying in state. It is frightening. This is not the familiar Uncle Isak but a distant menacing enemy who is living a secret life beyond insurmountable walls. ALEXANDER regards him with repugnance and slight fear. At the foot of the catafalque a camp bed stands crosswise. ARON is lying in it curled up. His face is waxen in the fluid light. His mouth is open and there are black shadows under the long quivering eyelashes. The dark hair over his forehead is damp and his hands are half open. He could be a child or an old man. ALEXANDER gazes at all this but his need makes itself urgently felt and he wakens out of his thoughts)

ALEXANDER   I can't hold it another second. I'll widdle on that palm tree. It looks dry and withered and in need of some water.

(In a corner stands a yellowing palm in a bulging jardinière. ALEXANDER has a long, luxurious pee. ISAK JACOBI snores. ARON lies like the dead. As ALEXANDER pees he realizes that he is lost and won't be able to find his way back to his room)

ALEXANDER   It's not going to be so easy to find my way back.

(He opens a door and knows he is going the wrong way. A cold shiver of uneasiness makes him sit down on the nearest chair. He draws up his bare feet, which have become rather dirty, and shuts his eyes tightly to press back the panic or the tears. When he opens them his father is standing in front of him, looking at him with kindly, worried eyes. ALEXANDER is not afraid, nor is he particularly pleased. He looks away.)

OSCAR *sits down carefully in a small armchair, thus making himself smaller than his son)*

OSCAR   It's not my fault everything has gone wrong. I'm powerless, Alexander. It is terrible to stand on one side and watch you all being tormented. I don't know what sins I committed in life to be forced to live in a hell like this.

ALEXANDER   You can keep away like all the rest.

OSCAR   Most can. I can't.

ALEXANDER   You always said that when you die you come to God. So it isn't true?

OSCAR   I cannot leave you.

ALEXANDER   Since you can't help us you might as well think of yourself and clear off to Heaven or wherever you're going.

OSCAR   I lived my life with you children and Emilie. Death makes no difference.

ALEXANDER   Well anyway, it's not my worry.

OSCAR   Why are you so angry, Alexander?

ALEXANDER   Hah.

OSCAR   I haven't done you any harm.

ALEXANDER   I may have liked you when you were alive —I think I did at any rate. Fanny and Amanda liked you better than I did because you always gave them presents.

OSCAR   I gave you presents too.

ALEXANDER   Oh, I know you did. But I never knew where I was with you, Papa. You always shilly-shal-

lied. Mama and Grandmamma decided everything.
You just made a fool of yourself and it made me
ashamed when you wandered about asking everyone's advice. You never said straight out what you
thought. Then you died. And now you're wandering
about in exactly the same way as when you were
alive. You say you feel sorry for us. That's just talk,
Papa. Why can't you go to God and tell him to kill
the bishop? That is his department. Or is it so that
God doesn't give a damn about you? About any of
us? Have you even *seen* God over there on the other
side? I bet you haven't even found out what chance
there is of getting close to God. You've just drifted
around as usual, worrying about us children and
Mama.

OSCAR   My father also thought I was a weakling.

(OSCAR *says this in a small voice, his face turned away.
Large tears are trickling down his round cheeks.* ALEX-
ANDER *is about to say something but thinks better of it. He
is silent and embittered. At last he speaks straight out into
the room*)

ALEXANDER   Not a bastard has a thought in his head.

OSCAR   You must be gentle with people, Alexander.

ALEXANDER   Idiots. The whole lot of them.

OSCAR   By and by you will understand—

ALEXANDER   That's just a lot of talk. I don't believe it.
"By and by you will understand." What damned by
and by? I see clearly. People are absurd and I dislike
them.

(*He screws up his eyes. When he opens them his father has
gone. The dawn light is cold and he shivers*)

V

(The same night and the same time in the bishop's palace. The clock in the tower strikes once more, four booming strokes. A bleak dawn light rises slowly behind the brick mass of the cathedral. EMILIE *is sitting in the dining room at one end of the table. She has a cup of hot broth in front of her. Her body is swollen with pregnancy, her cheeks are pale and sunken, her lips are dry and tight. She has let herself be carried away by strange thoughts and pictures; her eyes are fixed on the flickering morning light. A paraffin lamp is burning with a sallow glow. Footsteps are heard and a door opens)*

EDVARD   Aren't you coming to bed? The clock just struck four.

EMILIE   I can't sleep.

EDVARD   Nor can I.

EMILIE   I have been with Elsa. She is very ill. We ought to send for Doctor Fürstenberg.

EDVARD   He's coming tomorrow morning.

EMILIE   She's dying.

EDVARD   God's will be done. *(Pause)* What are you drinking?

EMILIE   I have made myself a cup of hot broth. It helps against insomnia.

EDVARD   May I have some?

EMILIE   *(With a smile)*   But of course.

(She pushes the cup over to BISHOP VERGÉRUS, *who sips the broth. He passes his hand across his forehead and*

cheeks. His eyes are inflamed and dull with weeping and insomnia)

EDVARD   Won't you forgive me?

EMILIE   I'm staying with you, am I not?

EDVARD   This sudden yielding. I don't understand it.

EMILIE   Drink it while it's hot.

EDVARD   What if you poisoned me.

EMILIE   Would it be so surprising?

EDVARD   No.

(He gulps the broth, puts down the cup, rubs his face again, lays his hand on the table, and spreads out his fingers. It is a broad white hand with knobby joints and wrinkled skin)

EMILIE   You demand that the children shall come back?

EDVARD   Yes.

EMILIE   In that case the position is hopeless.

EDVARD   I don't care about what is hopeless or not. I care only for what is right.

EMILIE   Isn't that Elsa calling?

EDVARD   Stay there. I'll go in and see to her.

(He tramps through the rooms in his coarse threadbare dressing gown, his footsteps heavy and clumsy. He is a clumping shadow, a brooding despair, a condemned man two hours before his execution. [Nothing is what it should be any more but he does not complain. It is no good blaming God or EMILIE *or circumstances.* BISHOP VERGÉRUS *blames himself.] He opens the door of* ELSA's *room. She is lying like a swollen*

whale against a mountain of pillows. Her face is ravaged and discolored, her eyes are popping out of their sockets, her mouth is wide-open)

EDVARD Did you call, Elsa?

ELSA Yes.

EDVARD Can I help you?

ELSA It's so dark.

(EDVARD *lifts the bedside table with the burning paraffin lamp and places it right against the bed, so that Miss Bergius can see the lamp and reach it with her hand. He bends over her and breathes in the stench of her mortal dread. Then he goes out suddenly, leaving the door ajar. She moans softly, almost resignedly, lifts her right hand with a great effort, and lays it on the hot bright shade of the lamp. [There is no counsel for the defense, who, orally or in writing, has a mind to plead* ELSA BERGIUS's *cause. She is repulsive, she is rotting, a parasite, a monster. Her part will soon be played out. She is a loaf that hasn't risen in the world's batch and it is no use wasting pity on such an utter failure.]*

EMILIE *is sitting on the bed in her grubby nightgown. She has drawn a shawl round her shoulders and her hands are resting against her thighs.* EDVARD *is standing by the window, drinking the last of the broth)*

EMILIE Can you see what the time is? My watch has stopped.

EDVARD Almost half-past four.

EMILIE It was a long night.

EDVARD You should try to get some sleep.

EMILIE My legs are hurting. They are swollen and aching.

(Husband and wife are silent. The immobility is complete. The seconds and the minutes crawl through the room. This is the end)

EDVARD   I have heard that the cosmos is expanding. The celestial bodies are hurtling away from each other at dizzy speed. The universe is exploding and we exist at the very moment of explosion.

*(*EMILIE *says nothing, looks at him)*

EDVARD   To "understand." What a misused word. I understand. I understand what you mean. I understand how you feel. Lies.

*(*EMILIE *says nothing, looks at him)*

EDVARD   You once said that you were always changing masks, so that finally you didn't know who you were. *(Pause)* I have only one mask. But it is branded into my flesh. If I try to tear it off—

*(*EMILIE *says nothing, looks at him.* EDVARD *sits down on his side of the bed.* EMILIE *turns her back on him. She is still motionless, as in a stifling tension)*

EDVARD   I always thought people liked me. I saw myself as wise, broad-minded, and fair. I had no idea that anyone was capable of hating me.

EMILIE   *I* don't hate you.

EDVARD   Your son does.

EMILIE   That is true.

EDVARD   I am afraid of him.

VI

Alexander has perhaps been asleep for a few moments, perhaps he is still asleep, perhaps this is a dream. It may also be that he has merely closed his eyes, that everything that now follows is not a fantasy or a dream at all, but reality. When, not very often, he occasionally thinks back on his three experiences he still cannot make up his mind whether to make light of them or whether to regard them as crucial. At all events reflections are futile and are not seen on film, so the two remaining experiences will be related just as they passed through Alexander's consciousness. It therefore doesn't matter whether he had been asleep, whether he was still asleep, or whether he had merely closed his eyes.

(ALEXANDER *hears a faint dragging sound and opens his eyes. A door far away at the other end of the room has been partly opened. Grasping the handle is a frighteningly big hand followed by a measureless wrist, which vanishes into a wide sleeve of thick dark red material.* ALEXANDER *hears a loud, calm breathing behind the door. He knows that a giant is hiding out in the darkness of the passage. He is paralyzed with elementary horror. The hair at the back of his neck bristles, his heart stops beating, his lips are cold, and his face is stiff.*

The door creaks softly and is pushed open wider. Something red and shapeless can be glimpsed, billowing. The white hand on the door is like a huge dying animal. Another door opens and behind it is a flickering light that runs effortlessly over the threshold and floats quickly up to the ceiling with a tinkling laugh. A face is faintly visible right inside the glow, the face of a laughing girl. It is framed by red hair. Suddenly the light goes out and the figure has vanished)

ALEXANDER   This is the end of me. Isn't it?

(A soft many-voiced laugh echoes under the ceiling and out of the dark corners. The white hand moves in a semicircle and the shapeless red thing billows)

ALEXANDER   Who's behind the door?

VOICE   It is God behind the door.

ALEXANDER   Can't you come out?

VOICE   No one living may see God's face.

ALEXANDER   What do you want with me?

VOICE   I only want to prove that I exist.

ALEXANDER   I am very grateful. Thank you.

VOICE   For me you are merely an insignificant little grain of dust. Did you know that?

ALEXANDER   No.

VOICE   Besides, you are unkind to your sisters and your parents, you are insolent to your teachers, and you think nasty thoughts. I don't really know why I let you live, Alexander.

ALEXANDER   No.

VOICE   *Holiness!* Alexander!

ALEXANDER   What?

VOICE   Holiness! The cow that tossed the dog, that worried the cat, that killed the rat, and so on. Do you understand what I mean?

ALEXANDER   I don't think I do.

VOICE   God is the world and the world is God. That's all there is to it.

ALEXANDER   Please forgive me, but if it's as you say, then I am God too.

VOICE   You are not God at all, you are just a stuck-up little brat.

ALEXANDER   I can't see that I'm any more stuck-up than God is. I'd be grateful if God would prove the opposite.

VOICE   *Love*, Alexander!

ALEXANDER   What love?

VOICE   I am speaking of *My* Love. God's love. God's love for Man. *(Pause)* Well?

ALEXANDER   Oh yes, I've heard of that love.

VOICE   Is there anything greater than love?

ALEXANDER   Well, if there is it would be His Grace the bishop's cockstand. I can't think of anything else as I'm only ten years old and haven't much experience.

VOICE   That was the right answer but a pretty cheeky one. Would you like me to perform a miracle?

ALEXANDER   What can you do?

VOICE   I am almighty. Have you forgotten?

ALEXANDER   I haven't forgotten but I don't believe it, because you're always harping on being almighty. If you really were almighty it would be so obvious that neither you nor the bishop would have to prove your omnipotence every Sunday.

(The redness behind the door billows more violently, the hand stretches out, and the fingers move. It looks horrible. A dull roar spreads through the floorboards. The door is now thrown

wide-open, a gigantic figure with a swollen face falls out on to the floor, and from a hole in the ceiling ARON *jumps down in front of* ALEXANDER. *He is laughing)*

ARON   You believed it!

ALEXANDER   I saw from the start that it was a puppet.

ARON   No, you didn't. You were afraid.

ALEXANDER   I wasn't a damn bit afraid.

ARON *(Mimicking)*   "This is the end of me. Isn't it?"

(ALEXANDER *loses his temper and hits* ARON's *laughing mouth. There is a short and furious fight. After a few moments* ALEXANDER *is lying pinned to the floor with* ARON *sitting on his stomach)*

ALEXANDER   I give in. *(Sorrowfully)* I give in.

(ARON *smiles suddenly and pats his cheek)*

ARON   Don't cry, Alexander, I didn't mean to frighten you. At least not much. I've been sitting all night working on that puppet—there's a wealthy circus owner in England who is mad about our puppets. Then I heard you tiptoeing about. *(Listens)* Quiet. Do you hear? Now my brother Ismael is awake. Can you hear? He's singing. Poor Ismael! Human beings are more than he can bear. Sometimes he gets violent and then he's dangerous. Come along, we'll go and see him. The doctors say that his intelligence is far above the normal. He never stops reading. He's incredibly learned and knows everything by heart. Would you like a cup of coffee, Alexander? Or a slice of bread? Shall I heat some milk for you?

ALEXANDER   You said you had been up all night. But I saw you lying asleep in your uncle's bedroom.

ARON   There is much that is strange and cannot be explained. You notice that particularly when you dabble in magic. Have you seen our mummy? Look carefully, Alexander. Can you see it breathing? It has been dead for more than four thousand years but it breathes. I'll make the room dark. What do you see?

ALEXANDER   It's shining!

ARON   Yes. No one knows why it is luminous. Dozens of learned men have been here and examined the old lady both outside and inside, but they can't explain why she shines. Anything unintelligible makes people angry. It's much better to blame the apparatus and the mirrors and the projections. Then people start laughing and that's healthier from all points of view—particularly the financial one. My father and mother ran a conjurer's theater in Petersburg. That's why I know what I'm talking about. One evening, in the middle of the performance, a real ghost appeared, an aunt of my father's. She had died two days earlier. The ghost lost her way among the machines and the projectors. It was a fiasco and Papa had to refund the admission.

ALEXANDER   I know quite a bit about ghosts.

ARON   Uncle Isak says we are surrounded by realities, one outside the other. He says that there are swarms of ghosts, spirits, phantoms, souls, poltergeists, demons, angels, and devils. He says that the smallest pebble has a life of its own. *(Breaking off)* Would you like some more coffee, Alexander?

ALEXANDER   Yes, please.

ARON *(Pouring it out)*   Everything is alive. Everything is God or God's thought, not only what is good but also the cruelest things. What do *you* think?

ALEXANDER   If there *is* a God, then he's a shit and piss God and I'd like to kick him in the arse.

ARON *(Politely)*   I think your theory is very interesting, my dear Alexander. Moreover, it appears to be fairly well justified. I for my part am an atheist. If one has been brought up as a magician and has learnt all the tricks in childhood, then one can do without supernatural interference! A sorcerer like me prefers to show what is understandable; it is up to the spectators to provide what is not. Shall we take Ismael his breakfast? Come, Alexander! There's nothing wrong with your common sense, especially as you're only nine.

ALEXANDER   I shall be eleven in November.

VII

(At this very hour on this sultry September morning EDVARD *realizes that he has been given sleeping pills. He is still sitting on the edge of the bed with his face turned to the window and wearing his coarse dressing gown.* EMILIE *is standing quite still by the door)*

EMILIE   Your sister gave me a tube of bromide pills, as I couldn't sleep. I had put three in the broth. It was not my intention that you should drink it. When you went to see to Elsa I put another three pills in the cup.

EDVARD   Hell and damnation.

EMILIE   You will sleep soundly. When you wake up I shall be gone. I shall wash, comb my hair, and dress without any hurry. Then I shall go downstairs and unlock the front door. I am going back to my children, to the theater, to my house, and my family.

EDVARD   I love you!

EMILIE   In a few minutes you will be asleep. When you wake up you will be tormented by longing and loneliness. But such feelings pass, Edvard.

EDVARD   I shall be different and you will come back.

EMILIE   I will never come back.

EDVARD   I shall pursue you from town to town. I shall poison your life and ruin your children's future.

EMILIE   Poor Edvard, you don't know what you're saying any longer.

EDVARD   I am awake. I am horribly awake.

(Half-blind and enraged, he gets up and stumbles toward her, groping for her arm. She avoids him. He tries to focus his gaze on her. Hollow, convulsive sobs shake him and tears keep filling his inflamed eyes)

EDVARD   Help me into bed at least. I can't see any more. And I feel dizzy.

(He stands with outstretched arms and closed eyes in the middle of the room, illuminated by the oppressive dawn. EMILIE forgets herself for a moment and steps forward to help him. Suddenly she stops, out of reach)

EDVARD   Are you there? I can't see you. I can't see.

EMILIE   I am here.

EDVARD   Help me.

EMILIE   I don't dare to help you.

(The hollow tearing sobs, the unseeing eyes, the slobbering half-open mouth, the outstretched arms, the bent tottering figure with the head poked forward. The dark beds with their puffy bolsters, the Crucified grimacing from pain, the heavy curtains, the shabby armchairs, the leaden sickly dawn which is neither shadow nor light. EMILIE *sees all this; for the rest of her life she will see the image of this moment, she will hear the crying and the panting, she will feel the pounding of her heart and smell the dust and the cold sweat of fear. This very picture, this very moment)*

VIII

*(*ARON *opens the forbidden door.* ALEXANDER *enters a long narrow room with a curtainless window at the end. In the middle of the floor stands a rough table and a broken armchair. The walls are lined with shelves, which are cluttered with books, newspapers, and piles of papers. On a camp bed with dirty bedclothes lies a boy of about sixteen. He has a round pale face, curly auburn hair, and narrow pale blue eyes. His movements are gracefully girlish and his voice light and a trifle hoarse. He is wearing a black suit much too small for him and a scarf; he has no waistcoat and his shirt is stained. His hands are chubby with short fingers. Instead of shoes he has thick gray socks. He regards* ARON *and* ALEXANDER *with an amused expression and does not move off the bed)*

ARON   Good morning, Ismael. We've brought your breakfast. This is my friend, Alexander Ekdahl.

(ISMAEL *rises quickly from the bed and goes up to* ALEX-ANDER *He lays a hand on his shoulder and studies him with his pale blue eyes. Then he nods in confirmation and smiles without smiling*)

ISMAEL   An idiot can see that Alexander isn't well. Leave us alone, Aron. You needn't worry, I shan't eat him up, even if he does look appetizing. Don't forget to lock the door on the outside. You can come back in half an hour. Go now, Aron!

(ISMAEL *utters these last words with sudden and sharp impatience, though his lips are still smiling their thin smile*)

ARON   Uncle Isak wouldn't like it if . . .

ISMAEL   Uncle Isak is an old goat and will never know about Alexander's visit. Go now!

(ARON *goes reluctantly and locks the door behind him.* ISMAEL *sips the hot coffee and holds out the mug to* ALEXANDER)

ALEXANDER   No, thank you.

ISMAEL   My name is Ismael, you know that already. "And he will be a wild man; his hand will be against every man, and every man's hand against him." I'm considered dangerous, that's why I'm locked in. I don't really mind.

ALEXANDER   In what way are you dangerous?

ISMAEL   I have awkward talents.

ALEXANDER   Awkward?

ISMAEL   Write your name on this piece of paper; it's ordinary wrapping paper. Here's a pencil. I'm afraid it's rather blunt but it will do. There. Alexander Ekdahl. Now read what you have written.

ALEXANDER   "Ismael Retzinsky."

ISMAEL   Perhaps we are the same person. Perhaps we have no limits; perhaps we flow into each other, stream through each other, boundlessly and magnificently. You bear terrible thoughts; it is almost painful to be near you. At the same time it is enticing. Do you know why?

ALEXANDER   I don't think I want to know.

ISMAEL   Evil thoughts have a considerable enticement. Most people cannot materialize it and that is perhaps fortunate for mankind. Anyway, it's all primitive and barbarous! For example, you make an image of someone you dislike and stick pins in it. It's rather a clumsy method when you think of the swift and straight ways that evil thoughts can go.

ALEXANDER   I don't think I want to talk to you about this.

ISMAEL   You're a strange little person, Alexander. You don't want to talk about what you are thinking of every moment.

ALEXANDER   If that's so—Yes, it's true.

ISMAEL   Tell me what you're thinking.

(ALEXANDER *shakes his head*)

ISMAEL   You have in mind a man's death. Wait a moment. Don't say anything. I know whom you are thinking of: A tall man with fair graying hair and beard—correct me if I'm wrong—he has clear blue eyes and a bony face, he is broad-shouldered—correct me if I'm wrong—he is asleep and dreaming that he is kneeling at the altar. Above the altar hangs the Crucified Prophet. In his dream he gets up and cries out through the huge cathedral: "Holy, holy, holy is the Lord of Hosts: The whole earth is full of his glory." It is taking place out there in the darkness. No one answers him, not even a laugh.

ALEXANDER   Please don't talk like that.

ISMAEL   It is not I talking. It is yourself. I am saying your mental pictures aloud. I am repeating your thoughts. The truth about the world is the truth about God. You are not to hesitate. He is sound asleep, plagued by nightmares. Give me your hand, Alexander. It isn't really necessary but it's safer. The doors are to be thrown open—a scream is to go through the house.

ALEXANDER   I don't want to! I don't want to!

ISMAEL   It is too late. I know your wish. *(Laughs)* A little boy like you nursing such hatred, such horrible wishes! *(Teasingly)* Your thin little chest could burst. Don't be afraid, Alexander. All you have to do is not to hesitate at the last moment; so I'll hold you in my arms. You have only one way to go and I am coming with you. I obliterate myself; I merge into you, my little child. Don't be afraid. I am with you; I am your guardian angel. The time is five o'clock in the morning and the sun has just risen. The doors are thrown open —no, wait. First a scream, a horrible scream echoing through the house, a shapeless burning figure moving across the floor—shrieking . . .

ALEXANDER   I don't want to! Let me go, *let me go!*

(ALEXANDER tries to free himself from ISMAEL's embrace but he cannot move; he cannot even scream. Now he clearly sees the burning figure as it staggers and howls)

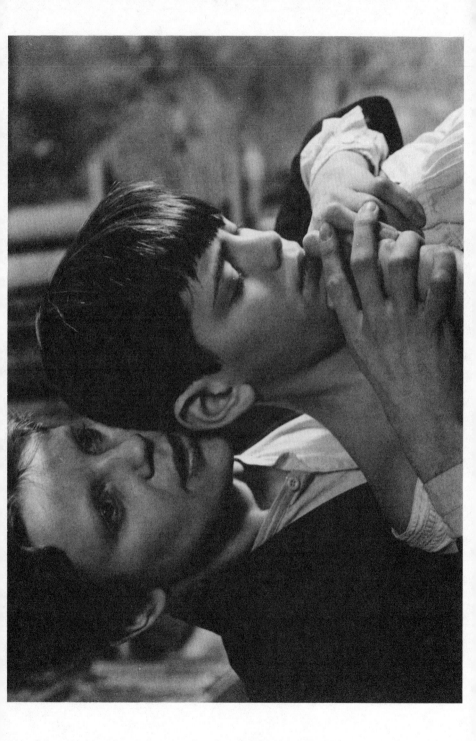

IX

EMILIE   What has happened?

POLICE SUPERINTENDENT   Your husband, His Grace the
bishop, lost his life this morning in terrible circumstances. We think we can make clear the course of
events in detail. Miss Elsa Bergius, who was gravely
ill, lay in bed. On her bedside table stood a lighted
paraffin lamp. By an unlucky chance the lamp fell on
to the bed, igniting not only the bedclothes but also
Miss Bergius's hair and nightgown. Burning like a
torch, the sick woman rushed through the house and
chanced to make her way into His Grace, the bishop's
bedchamber. According to His Grace's sister, Miss
Henrietta Vergérus, His Grace was in a heavy sleep
after drinking a soporific, which you, Mrs. Vergérus,
had given him earlier in the evening. After a violent
altercation with your husband, you left the house at
twenty minutes past four in the morning. Miss Bergius flung herself on the sleeping man, thus igniting
his bedclothes and nightshirt. His Grace woke up
and succeeded in freeing himself from the dying
woman, who was still burning, but could not extin-
guish the flames that were now engulfing himself. Old
Mrs. Vergérus found her son with the top of his
body severely burnt and his face charred. He showed
faint signs of life and kept calling out that his agony
was unendurable. Ten minutes later the doctor and
ambulance arrived on the scene, but by then His
Grace had already been released from his suffering
and had breathed his last. Although I cannot over-
look the fact that the sleeping draft you gave him
possibly made the disaster worse, at the same time I
cannot attach any serious importance to it. I must

characterize what happened as a dreadful combination of particularly unfortunate circumstances and therefore beg to offer my deep and sincere condolences.

X

(Two days after BISHOP VERGÉRUS's *appalling decease* EMILIE *and her children visit the theater. They are in mourning, and the widow is heavily veiled. It is early in the afternoon and a few rays of autumn sunlight shine in through the cracks in the shutters. The sleepy working light flickers over the stage; the auditorium is in darkness. The actors move about like groping shadows in the dusty half-light)*

HARALD MORSING   Madame, I had the honor to wait upon you yesterday, but your maid showed me the door with an offensive message.

HANNA SCHWARTZ   Monsieur le Marquis, I blush for your presumption and can only deplore the fact that my servants this morning were unable to show you the door again. You say that you love me, sir. In that case have the goodness to spare me your presence, which, I own, arouses vexation in me, not to say anger, at the remembrance of the humiliation you caused me in the presence of Her Majesty the queen.

MIKAEL BERGMAN *(Entering)*   Why, Monsieur le Marquis, to what do we owe the honor of such an early visit?

FILIP LANDAHL *(Aside)* A desperate surprise in very truth! How will this turn out? I am on tenterhooks!

HARALD MORSING Monsieur le Comte!

MIKAEL BERGMAN Monsieur le Marquis!

HARALD MORSING Only the thought of the blood you have shed for your king, sir, prevents me from instantly and with all my power throwing back in your face the infamy you have committed against the marquise. Spare this noble lady the shame that—

PROMPTER *(Blowing his nose)* —you have brought down over my house.

HARALD MORSING —that you have brought down over my house. *(To Filip Landahl)* As if it weren't enough that this is the worst piffle ever written in French, the translation is vile, Mr. Landahl. I tell you that candidly, although I know you have gone to great pains.

FILIP LANDAHL I know it has been done in haste, Mr. Morsing, but we are in a crisis.

HARALD MORSING Formerly we played Shakespeare, my good sir. We played the great Molière, we were even bold enough to let Henrik Ibsen's voice be heard.

FILIP LANDAHL Public taste, Mr. Morsing! Audiences no longer wish to hear the songs of the giants; they are content with the squeaking of dwarfs. No one bothers about our theater any more, neither the general public nor the Ekdahl family. The takings drop and our actors feel the draft.

(HANNA SCHWARTZ and MIKAEL BERGMAN have sat down dejectedly on a the wooden sofa without arms. They hold each other's hand and sit there gloomily)

EMILIE *(Whispering)* Hanna!

(HANNA can see EMILIE and the children in the semidarkness of the wings. She utters a joyous exclamation. The two men break off their argument and turn round. MIKAEL BERGMAN stands up with a look of astonishment. No one moves. Then EMILIE opens her arms and HANNA embraces her. Everyone starts weeping with excitement. They kiss one another, stroke each other's hands and cheeks, laugh and talk quietly, as if anxious not to frighten the moment away)

FILIP LANDAHL   I have no words. I have no words.

HARALD MORSING   Dear Mrs. Ekdahl, dear, dear Mrs. Ekdahl.

MIKAEL BERGMAN   I don't know why I am so damned moved.

HANNA SCHWARTZ   You'll stay with us now, won't you?

Epilogue

During the winter Emilie and Maj have each been delivered of a baby of female sex, to the great joy not only of the mothers but also of the brothers and sisters, of the excessively proud Gustav Adolf, and particularly of Helena, who, contrary to her wont, had been poorly and somewhat melancholy during the autumn. With a true Ekdahl feeling for festivity it has been decided to have a double christening in lilac time.

(The winter has at last been conquered and the early summer is in full bloom. It is a sunny day after a gentle shower of

rain. The mothers themselves hold their babies at the christen-
ing, which takes place in EMILIE*'s apartment. The officiating*
CLERGYMAN *is an elderly vicar, who, lavishly bribed by*
GUSTAV ADOLF, *shuts both eyes to the dubious lineage of one*
of the infants. The entire family is of course present and the
actors from the theater have been invited.

The ladies wear large flower-decked hats, the men formal
morning dress, and ALEXANDER *is miserable in a white sailor*
suit. VEGA *and* ESTER *preen themselves in newly made gray*
silk dresses and the other servants have dolled themselves up
according to taste and means. Even before the ceremony,
champagne has been drunk and spirits are high, almost frivo-
lous. Dinner is served in HELENA*'s large dining room. The*
huge table is covered with a red cloth and a wealth of flowers;
the silver candelabra and the chandeliers glitter in the sun-
light, the orchestra from the theater plays waltzes, and the
two infants rest in their cots on a special platform decorated
with lilacs and pink roses. Many feel called upon to make a
speech, especially GUSTAV ADOLF, *who makes two.*

GUSTAV ADOLF   My dear, dear friends. I am moved more
than I can say. Dear friends, dearest Mama, my greatly
loved wife Alma, my darling Emilie, more beautiful
than ever, my wonderful children Petra and Jenny,
and little Miss Helena Viktoria, *no less,* lying there as
good as gold in her cot, and dear Maj, whom I am so
very fond of! Not forgetting my incomparable brother
and his sweet wife and my highly esteemed friend Isak
Jacobi, who has rendered immeasurable service to this
family, dear Vega and Ester, and all you good friends
who so loyally help us up the hill of life. Last but not
least, those dear and admired and greatly talented and
superb actors, Mr. Landahl, Miss Schwartz, Mr. Morsing, and Mr. Bergman. If I could I would throw my
arms round you all in a vast embrace and I would
plant a kiss of affection on your brows, a kiss that,

more than any words, would tell you of my happiness
and my love. We are all together again now. Our little
world has closed round us in security, wisdom, and
order after a time of horror and confusion. The shadows of death have been routed, winter has been put to
flight, and joy has returned to our hearts. Now I must
lift Miss Helena Viktoria up from her cot—is that
allowed? I knew it would be. Amanda, go and get little
Aurora and nurse her in your lap; she is not to feel
forgotten on this happy day, the best day of my life.
Now I'm going to make a speech. Look, she's laughing
at me, my daughter Helena Viktoria. Go on, laugh at
your old father and never mind what he says. It's all
nonsense! *(His eyes fill with tears)* My wisdom is simple,
and there are no doubt people who despise it. But I
don't give a damn. Forgive me, Mama. I see you raising your right eyebrow; you think your eldest son is
talking too much. Don't worry, I'll be brief. Well now,
we Ekdahls have not come into the world to see
through it, never think that. We are not equipped for
such excursions. We might just as well ignore the big
things. We must live in the little, the little world. We
shall be content with that and cultivate it and make
the best of it. Suddenly death strikes, suddenly the
abyss opens, suddenly the storm howls and disaster is
upon us—all that we *know*. But let us not think of all
that unpleasantness. We love what we can understand.
We Ekdahls like our subterfuges. Rob a man of his
subterfuges and he goes mad and begins hitting out.
(Laughs) Damn it all, people must be intelligible, or we
don't dare either to love them or speak ill of them. We
must be able to grasp the world and reality, so that we
can complain of its monotony with a clear conscience.
Dear, splendid actors and actresses, we *need* you all the
same. It is you who are to give us our supernatural
shudders and still more our mundane amusements.

The world is a den of thieves and night is falling. Soon it will be the hour for robbers and murderers. Evil is breaking its chains and goes through the world like a mad dog. The poisoning affects us all, without exception, us Ekdahls and everyone else. No one escapes, not even Helena Viktoria or little Aurora over there in Amanda's lap. *(Weeps)* So it shall be. Therefore let us be happy while we are happy, let us be kind, generous, affectionate, and good. Therefore it is necessary, and not in the least shameful, to take pleasure in *the little world,* good food, gentle smiles, fruit-trees in bloom, waltzes. And now, my dearest friends, my dearest brothers and sisters, I've done talking and you can take it for what you like—the effusions of an uncouth restaurant owner or the pitiful babbling of an old man. It doesn't matter to me, I don't care one way or the other. I am holding a little empress in my arms. It is tangible yet immeasurable. One day she will prove me wrong, one day she will rule over not only the *little* world but over—everything! Everything!

(He raises Helena Viktoria as if she were a goblet and kisses her on the stomach.

About ten in the evening the festivities die down and EMILIE *withdraws to breast-feed her daughter. She is reclining comfortably in an easy chair, her legs on a padded stool. She is wearing a wide green dressing gown. The nursemaid is hovering shyly in the doorway. She is a girl of about twenty, thin as a lath, with thick brown hair and large dark eyes. Her name is* ROSA.

EMILIE *lifts Aurora to her shoulder and pats her on the bottom)*

EMILIE   She usually goes to sleep with this feed. *(Prattles with her daughter)* There, my poppet! Be a good girl now, so that mama can go to bed. I think you've had all you want.

ROSA I'll take her.

EMILIE Thank you, Rosa.

ROSA Good night, madam.

EMILIE Good night, Rosa. How do you like it here?

ROSA I've never had such a nice place in all my life. Everyone's so kind. Especially Mr. Ekdahl. He must be a good man; he's ever so kind to everybody.

EMILIE Yes, he's a good man, and he is particularly kind to young girls, so you watch out, Rosa.

ROSA *(Ambiguously)* Lawks!

EMILIE Good night, Rosa.

(EMILIE *goes to say good night to the children. She moves through the apartment, enjoying the evening light and the stillness.* GUSTAV ADOLF, *rather tipsy, is sitting in the drawing room with a grog)*

EMILIE Aren't you going to bed?

GUSTAV ADOLF Hahahahaha!

EMILIE Blow the lamp out when you go.

GUSTAV ADOLF *(Saluting)* Very good, sir! Hahahaha!

(In *the nursery there is mysterious activity. The blinds are pulled down, blankets are spread over the floor, candles are burning in front of the blankets, and there are screens at the sides.* AMANDA *is gliding through the room with a sheet over her nightgown.* FANNY *and* JENNY *are perched on two chairs, holding each other's hands.* ALEXANDER *is lying stretched out on the floor with a handkerchief over his face)*

FANNY Greetings, all-powerful king, emperor of all the worlds! *(Bows to* AMANDA)

JENNY *(Squeaking)*   Don't you think he seems rather pale?

FANNY   He seems almost transparent.

JENNY   If you ask me, he doesn't look nice at all. And he smells!

ALEXANDER *(Under the handkerchief)*   I'm dying!

FANNY   Now I can see his empty eye sockets. Ugh!

JENNY *(Squeaking)*   And I think his head is empty. Ugh!

(EMILIE, *unnoticed, watches the awful spectacle.* AMANDA *checks herself in the middle of a movement and, without losing her dignity, turns to her mother and explains that they are rehearsing a play that* ALEXANDER *has written and that they don't want to be disturbed)*

EMILIE   Well, be careful of the candles, and don't stay up too late.

(EMILIE *shuts the door carefully and can now hear horrible gurgling sounds from the dying man and frightened screams from the living. Death has taken shape in the nursery.*

EMILIE *passes again through the dining room.* ALMA *has just heaved* GUSTAV ADOLF *out of the chair and they are having a friendly bicker.* GUSTAV ADOLF *is assuring* ALMA *that he is quite sober, but she does not believe him for a moment. He doesn't want to go to bed, saying that they should wind up the festive day with a bottle of champagne.* ALMA *assures him that no one feels like drinking champagne at this time of evening but that she will give him a ham sandwich and a glass of beer if he goes with her down to their apartment)*

GUSTAV ADOLF   I'm sure Emilie would like some champagne. We'll drink to the health of our daughters.

EMILIE   Go to bed now, Gusten.

GUSTAV ADOLF   I am so bloody happy.

ALMA   That's good, Gusten, but tomorrow's another day and you'll have a headache.

GUSTAV ADOLF   Now we are together again.

EMILIE *(To* ALMA*)*   I'm going to the country tomorrow to speak to the workmen. Can I do anything for you? I'll be there until Thursday.

ALMA   Then I'll try and come out on Tuesday.

GUSTAV ADOLF   Don't you think I have the best wife in the world?

EMILIE   Much better than you deserve.

GUSTAV ADOLF   And the prettiest mistress to be found anywhere. A real little poppet.

ALMA   Are you leaving early tomorrow?

EMILIE   Not until two o'clock.

ALMA   Good night, Emilie. *(Kiss)*

EMILIE   Good night, Alma. *(Kiss)*

GUSTAV ADOLF   When I see you I want to cry with joy. To think that you're back with us again!

EMILIE   Good night, Gusten. Be a good boy now and remember that Alma needs to sleep.

GUSTAV ADOLF   I know what Alma needs!

(Laughing, they go out noisily and the staircase echoes with their clatter. EMILIE *leaves the hall door open to air the room and get rid of* GUSTAV ADOLF's *cigar smoke. When she gets back to her bedroom she finds she has visitors.* PETRA *and* MAJ *sit waiting for her, tense and serious)*

PETRA   We want to move to Stockholm.

MAJ   A friend of Petra's . . .

PETRA   Marianne Egerman, you know.

MAJ   . . . is going to open a milliner's shop . . .

PETRA   . . . and wants us to come to help her . . .

MAJ   . . . and we'd like to very much . . .

PETRA   . . . awfully much, in fact . . .

MAJ   . . . but we have a problem . . .

PETRA   Papa wants to buy that coffee shop for Maj.

MAJ   He's so kind *(Begins to weep)*

PETRA   But he's always telling Maj what to do, and she has had enough.

MAJ   He's so kind, it's hopeless.

PETRA   Maj wants to live her own life and do what *she* wants for herself and her child.

MAJ   I don't know what to do.

PETRA   We've spoken to Grandmamma and she thinks as we do.

MAJ   We've spoken to Alma too.

PETRA   Mama was awfully upset at first and said we couldn't do that to Papa.

MAJ   Then she calmed down and said that life must go on and that one shouldn't force one's children.

PETRA   Though she was awfully sorry for Papa's sake. You must think of yourself first. After all, Papa's an old man. Isn't he, Aunt Emilie?

EMILIE   Go to bed now. I'll have a word with Grand-mamma.

(The girls go out whispering. PETRA *affectionate, consoling* MAJ, *who is weeping, her curly red head leaning against* PETRA'*s ample bosom. It is still light outside the windows and a blackbird is practicing an aria.* EMILIE *is about to pull down the blind to make night definite but remains standing with her eyes on the pale evening sky and her hands clasped over what was her pregnant belly. "That's how it is," she says aloud to herself, "that's how it is")*

EMILIE   Poor Gustav Adolf. Poor numskull. But he has only himself to blame—or has he? Has any single person himself to blame or must we *all* blame ourselves? *(Gives a rueful little laugh)* It's a May evening and here I am alone talking to myself and I'll be forty-one next week. When Mama was forty her hair had gone white and she had chronic catarrh. Well, that's how it is. In the middle of life we're already at the end.

(She makes a face of annoyance at the mirror and thinks it came off rather well. Her decision to return to the theater is confirmed. She hunts in her little escritoire, *finds the book with red covers and gold-tooling, wraps her dressing gown around her, throws a shawl round her shoulders, and goes through the jib-door of the dining room into* HELENA'*s apartment.)*

EMILIE   I want to confer with you.

HELENA   Is it anything serious? Oh, I know. The girls want to move to Stockholm. What do you think?

EMILIE   Do you need to ask?

HELENA   Although I'm not exactly rolling in money at the moment (what that wretched theater cost us last winter), although as I said I'm rather hard up at present (Carl and Lydia have fleeced me—he keeps threatening to take his life—I'm his mother—good heavens what am I to do?), anyway although I'm short of cash I have promised the girls to pay their living expenses for the first year, not royally but unstintingly. They'll really have to get themselves some new clothes. They look like real little provincial roses, awfully pretty but not very well dressed.

EMILIE   Maj is worried about Gustav Adolf.

HELENA   Well, I never! His lordship my son has helped himself liberally to the good things of life and it's high time he realized he's on the wrong side of forty.

EMILIE   One other thing.

HELENA   Yes, you're quite right. Oscar on his deathbed asked you to take charge of the theater. I was there, I remember it very well.

EMILIE   Gustav Adolf will be terribly hurt.

HELENA   I can't understand this tender consideration for Gustav Adolf. He has managed the theater since your marriage, or rather mismanaged it to the point of ruin. Gusten has a good head for business but knows nothing about art. It is your theater, my dear Emilie, and it's time we made clear to our second-rate Napoleon that he's facing his Waterloo.

EMILIE   Then there's the problem of Amanda.

HELENA   What problem?

EMILIE   She has changed her mind about being a ballet dancer. She wants to stay here and matriculate.

HELENA   Oh, does she? Hm.

EMILIE   She has said nothing to you?

HELENA   No.

EMILIE   She wants to be a doctor.

HELENA   Would you like some liqueur?

EMILIE   Just a drop.

HELENA   Oho, so little Amanda Ekdahl wants to be a doctor!

EMILIE   You think we should back her up?

HELENA   That slip of a girl. *(Laughs)* Well, well!

EMILIE   I was uncertain, so I wanted to ask your advice.

HELENA   You? Uncertain!

EMILIE   I've got out of the way of making decisions.

HELENA   By the way, Emilie.

EMILIE   Yes?

HELENA   You know the chancellor of the university, don't you?

EMILIE   You mean Essias Ekberg? He's a very kind man and a keen theatergoer.

HELENA   Couldn't you have a word with him?

EMILIE   Don't you think Carl will get his research grant?

HELENA   Oh, yes, I think so, but one can never be sure.

EMILIE   Essias is calling to see me next week. I shall ask him to dinner.

HELENA   All the houses at Eknäset must be repaired. They're falling down. Nothing has been looked after since Oscar died. Last summer the wells kept drying up.

EMILIE   I'm going out there tomorrow. *(Shows* HELENA *the book with the red covers)* I'd like you to read a new play by August Strindberg.

HELENA   That abominable misogynist.

EMILIE   I'll put the book here.

HELENA   You have a plan?

EMILIE   There are parts for both of us.

HELENA   But my dear, I haven't appeared on a stage for—

EMILIE   All the more reason, Helena.

HELENA   Oh.

EMILIE   We must cherish our theater.

HELENA *(With a sigh)*   Yes, yes.

EMILIE   Well, it's bedtime. Good night, dearest.

HELENA   Good night, my little girl. *(They kiss)*

About the Author

Ingmar Bergman has been one of Europe's leading film and theater directors for thirty years. The first of his films to be known in America was *The Seventh Seal,* which was followed by such great films as *Smiles of a Summer Night, Persona, The Virgin Spring, Through a Glass Darkly, Cries and Whispers, Scenes from a Marriage, Face to Face, The Serpent's Egg, Autumn Sonata,* and most recently *From the Life of the Marionettes.*

Bergman has received every major American and European film prize and is considered by many to be the world's greatest living film director.